3,570 Real-world English Phrases for Speaking and Writing Practice

*

Volume 1

-by Everett Ofori

© Everett Ofori, 2018

All rights reserved. No part of this publication may be reproduced, stored in a retrieval system, or transmitted, in any form or by any means, without the prior permission in writing of Everett Ofori, or as expressly permitted by law, or under terms agreed with the appropriate reprographics rights organization.

Enquiries concerning reproduction outside the scope of the above should be sent to:

Everett Ofori
c/o Takarazuka University of Art and Design
Tokyo Campus Building 1F-123MBE
7-11-1 Nishi-Shinjuku
Shinjuku-ku
Tokyo, Japan 160-0023

10-digit ISBN: 1-894221-11-7
13-digit ISBN: 9781894221115

Other Books by Everett Ofori

1) Succeeding From the Margins of Canadian Society: A Strategic Resource for New Immigrants, Refugees and International Students. Written by Francis Adu-Febiri and Everett Ofori   © 2009 – ISBN 978-1-926585-27-7

2) Read Assure: Guaranteed Formula for Reading Success with Phonics.
Written by Everett Ofori   © 2010 – ISBN 978-1-926585-83-3

3) Guaranteed Formula for Writing Success.
Written by Everett Ofori   © 2011 – ISBN 978-1-926918-22-8

4) The Changing Japanese Woman: From *Yamatonadeshiko* to *YamatonadeGucci*.
Written by Everett Ofori   © 2013 – ISBN 13: 978-1894221047

5) Prepare for Greatness: How to Make Your Success Inevitable.
Written by Everett Ofori   © 2013 – ISBN 13: 978-0921143000

6) The Global Student's Companion: 10,001 Timeless Themes & Topics for Dialogue, Discussion & Debate Practice.
   Compiled by Everett Ofori   © 2015 – ISBN 13: 978-1-894221-02-3

7) Guaranteed Formula for Effective Business Writing.
   Written by Everett Ofori   © 2011 – ISBN 978-1894221108

8) Guaranteed Formula for Public Speaking Success.
   Written by Everett Ofori   © 2011 – ISBN 978-1894221078

9) English Language Mastermind: From Confident Communication to Higher Test Scores.
   Written by Everett Ofori   © 2011 – ISBN 978-1894221160

Introduction

Many English learners understand the importance of building their vocabulary, but simply memorizing words is, quite often, not enough. Memorized words are soon forgotten from lack of use. Learners who make it a habit of reading English books, however, are able to retain some of the words they learn as they come across some of the same words, again and again.

Even so, it is shortsighted to focus only on individual words. After all, words come in bundles, or collocations. Already, I have used the expression "come across." If you become familiar with words that usually go together, you can sometimes predict what a speaker is going to say. This gives you tremendous advantage when you are taking an English test.

A collocation, by the way, is defined by the Cambridge Dictionary as "a word or phrase that is often used with another word or phrase, in a way that sounds correct to people who have spoken the language all their lives...." While you should continue to build your vocabulary through extensive reading, you can give yourself additional practice in English speaking and writing by also paying attention to word clusters such as the ones offered in this book.

These phrases have been collected through hundreds of hours of listening to radio shows, television broadcasts, podcasts, university lectures and interviews. Phrases have also been culled from newspaper and magazine articles, as well as contemporary books of both fiction and nonfiction. Here's wishing you all the best in your continued efforts to become a more proficient user of the English language.

How to Use this Book

1	going to go	*(Write down the meaning of the phrase here)*
SS	*(Write down a sample sentence here. SS = Sample Sentence)*	
MS	*(Write down your own sentence here. MS = My Sentence)*	
2	by car	
SS		
MS		

The above pattern is used throughout the book.

If you are certain you know the meaning of a phrase, just go ahead and use that phrase in a sentence in the row labeled MS (My Sentence). If you are not sure about the meaning, search online using any major search engine and write down the meaning in the box to the right of the phrase.

To find a Sample Sentence (SS), you can type in the phrase in a search engine and add the name of a major newspaper, for example: "going to go" and NYTimes

Finally, get an English teacher or tutor to check if your sentences are correct. All the very best on your English learning journey.

1	going to go	
SS		
MS		
2	by car	
SS		
MS		
3	by bicycle	
SS		
MS		
4	take time to	
SS		
MS		
5	had a lovely	
SS		
MS		
6	during the trip	
SS		
MS		

7	there's a	
SS		
MS		
8	there's an	
SS		
MS		
9	there's no	
SS		
MS		
10	there's not a	
SS		
MS		
11	there are	
SS		
MS		
12	there are no	
SS		
MS		

13	on the table	
SS		
MS		
14	get into	
SS		
MS		
15	looked at	
SS		
MS		
16	throw out	
SS		
MS		
17	in the bus	
SS		
MS		
18	did not work out	
SS		
MS		

19	appears happy	
SS		
MS		
20	she herself	
SS		
MS		
21	particularly when	
SS		
MS		
22	may find	
SS		
MS		
23	might find	
SS		
MS		
24	will certainly find	
SS		
MS		

25	get used to	
SS		
MS		
26	near my house	
SS		
MS		
27	near to the store	
SS		
MS		
28	near the library	
SS		
MS		
29	went to	
SS		
MS		
30	stare at	
SS		
MS		

31	smile at	
SS		
MS		
32	evidence of	
SS		
MS		
33	snooze my alarm	
SS		
MS		
34	I sent	
SS		
MS		
35	I will send	
SS		
MS		
36	have sent	
SS		
MS		

37	came to	
SS		
MS		
38	looked into	
SS		
MS		
39	took X from	
SS		
MS		
40	give me	
SS		
MS		
41	did not see	
SS		
MS		
42	did not look at	
SS		
MS		

43	took a key out of	
SS		
MS		
44	threw X out of the window	
SS		
MS		
45	walked out of	
SS		
MS		
46	ran out of	
SS		
MS		
47	lived in	
SS		
MS		
48	last month	
SS		
MS		

49	said to	
SS		
MS		
50	told me to	
SS		
MS		
51	comply with	
SS		
MS		
52	bark at	
SS		
MS		
53	going to start	
SS		
MS		
54	in the evening	
SS		
MS		

55	in the afternoon	
SS		
MS		
56	in the morning	
SS		
MS		
57	last night	
SS		
MS		
58	this morning	
SS		
MS		
59	with the intention of	
SS		
MS		
60	did not go	
SS		
MS		

61	did not eat	
SS		
MS		
62	did not drink	
SS		
MS		
63	great with	
SS		
MS		
64	sit down with	
SS		
MS		
65	did not sit down with	
SS		
MS		
66	on the weekends	
SS		
MS		

67	every day	
SS		
MS		
68	always said	
SS		
MS		
69	always eat	
SS		
MS		
70	always take	
SS		
MS		
71	one of my friends is	
SS		
MS		
72	one of my teachers	
SS		
MS		

73	is funny	
SS		
MS		
74	was fun	
SS		
MS		
75	is lazy	
SS		
MS		
76	is hardworking	
SS		
MS		
77	do not like to	
SS		
MS		
78	did not like to	
SS		
MS		

79	on the sofa	
SS		
MS		
80	on the chair	
SS		
MS		
81	in the book	
SS		
MS		
82	in the newspaper	
SS		
MS		
83	in the magazine	
SS		
MS		
84	smaller than	
SS		
MS		

85	louder than	
SS		
MS		
86	bigger than	
SS		
MS		
87	faster than	
SS		
MS		
88	slower than	
SS		
MS		
89	go to school	
SS		
MS		
90	go to work	
SS		
MS		

91	go to the restaurant	
SS		
MS		
92	go to the store	
SS		
MS		
93	go home	
SS		
MS		
94	go to the hospital	
SS		
MS		
95	is cheap	
SS		
MS		
96	is expensive	
SS		
MS		

97	is quite cheap	
SS		
MS		
98	have been to X before	
SS		
MS		
99	have been to X many times	
SS		
MS		
100	fewer than	
SS		
MS		
101	have never been to	
SS		
MS		
102	not very	
SS		
MS		

103	finish school at	
SS		
MS		
104	finish work at	
SS		
MS		
105	am/is not allowed to	
SS		
MS		
106	finish lunch at	
SS		
MS		
107	looking for	
SS		
MS		
108	birthday is on	
SS		
MS		

109	work in a store	
SS		
MS		
110	work in an office	
SS		
MS		
111	work in a restaurant	
SS		
MS		
112	work in a hotel	
SS		
MS		
113	work on a ship	
SS		
MS		
114	always buy	
SS		
MS		

115	looked up to see	
SS		
MS		
116	looked down and saw	
SS		
MS		
117	play with	
SS		
MS		
118	study with	
SS		
MS		
119	work with	
SS		
MS		
120	dance with	
SS		
MS		

121	revel in the chance to	
SS		
MS		
122	wore a jacket	
SS		
MS		
123	very warm	
SS		
MS		
124	very cold	
SS		
MS		
125	nodded vigorously	
SS		
MS		
126	warm water	
SS		
MS		

127	tepid water	
SS		
MS		
128	lukewarm water	
SS		
MS		
129	took off my hat	
SS		
MS		
130	took off my gloves before	
SS		
MS		
131	answered the door	
SS		
MS		
132	a lot of sweets	
SS		
MS		

133	doesn't have	
SS		
MS		
134	a stick of gum	
SS		
MS		
135	a sheet of paper	
SS		
MS		
136	at the side of the house	
SS		
MS		
137	in front of the school	
SS		
MS		
138	behind the store	
SS		
MS		

139	pretty happy with	
SS		
MS		
140	not enough X for	
SS		
MS		
141	for one hour	
SS		
MS		
142	in one hour	
SS		
MS		
143	cannot find	
SS		
MS		
144	tired of	
SS		
MS		

145	a big hat	
SS		
MS		
146	a big house	
SS		
MS		
147	a hut	
SS		
MS		
148	in the shed	
SS		
MS		
149	irregular hours	
SS		
MS		
150	for a few hours	
SS		
MS		

151	is much better than before	
SS		
MS		
152	just a short distance from	
SS		
MS		
153	quite a long way from	
SS		
MS		
154	unhappy about	
SS		
MS		
155	happy about	
SS		
MS		
156	for a short time	
SS		
MS		

157	for a long time	
SS		
MS		
158	wait for	
SS		
MS		
159	often go to	
SS		
MS		
160	at the tennis court	
SS		
MS		
161	at the stadium	
SS		
MS		
162	at the baseball diamond	
SS		
MS		

163	at the soccer field	
SS		
MS		
164	scored a goal	
SS		
MS		
165	where is	
SS		
MS		
166	where are	
SS		
MS		
167	almost full	
SS		
MS		
168	almost empty	
SS		
MS		

169	got back late	
SS		
MS		
170	got back on time	
SS		
MS		
171	how many cups of	
SS		
MS		
172	how many pieces of	
SS		
MS		
173	it is not safe to	
SS		
MS		
174	it is dangerous to	
SS		
MS		

175	shut the door	
SS		
MS		
176	opened the window	
SS		
MS		
177	most of the time	
SS		
MS		
178	almost every day	
SS		
MS		
179	don't like	
SS		
MS		
180	don't want	
SS		
MS		

181	don't need	
SS		
MS		
182	listened to	
SS		
MS		
183	listened for	
SS		
MS		
184	drove to	
SS		
MS		
185	flew to	
SS		
MS		
186	walked to	
SS		
MS		

187	rode my bicycle to	
SS		
MS		
188	stopped at	
SS		
MS		
189	turn right at	
SS		
MS		
190	turn left at	
SS		
MS		
191	read a book	
SS		
MS		
192	read a magazine	
SS		
MS		

193	read a newspaper	
SS		
MS		
194	seldom go out to	
SS		
MS		
195	stopped to	
SS		
MS		
196	haven't told	
SS		
MS		
197	it isn't necessary to	
SS		
MS		
198	drive slowly	
SS		
MS		

199	drive fast	
SS		
MS		
200	last summer	
SS		
MS		
201	last winter	
SS		
MS		
202	last spring	
SS		
MS		
203	last autumn	
SS		
MS		
204	a village by the sea	
SS		
MS		

205	on the first day of school	
SS		
MS		
206	on the last day of	
SS		
MS		
207	a cold day	
SS		
MS		
208	a windy day	
SS		
MS		
209	a sunny day	
SS		
MS		
210	a cloudy day	
SS		
MS		

211	went to X alone	
SS		
MS		
212	go to X by myself	
SS		
MS		
213	go to X with	
SS		
MS		
214	might have been	
SS		
MS		
215	did not eat much	
SS		
MS		
216	did not talk much	
SS		
MS		

217	did not study much	
SS		
MS		
218	did not have much money	
SS		
MS		
219	didn't say anything to	
SS		
MS		
220	didn't say anything about	
SS		
MS		
221	bought a	
SS		
MS		
222	bought an	
SS		
MS		

223	as soon as possible	
SS		
MS		
224	have to stay away from	
SS		
MS		
225	ask (someone) some questions	
SS		
MS		
226	know the meaning of	
SS		
MS		
227	answered slowly	
SS		
MS		
228	answered quickly	
SS		
MS		

229	whisper to	
SS		
MS		
230	not going to buy	
SS		
MS		
231	not going to see	
SS		
MS		
232	not going to watch	
SS		
MS		
233	not going to do	
SS		
MS		
234	is like	
SS		
MS		

235	spoke to	
SS		
MS		
236	did not speak to	
SS		
MS		
237	the living room	
SS		
MS		
238	in the corridor	
SS		
MS		
239	woke up	
SS		
MS		
240	knocked at	
SS		
MS		

241	make noise	
SS		
MS		
242	made some noise	
SS		
MS		
243	made a lot of noise	
SS		
MS		
244	locked the door	
SS		
MS		
245	appeared to be	
SS		
MS		
246	work late	
SS		
MS		

247	wake up early	
SS		
MS		
248	a huge mistake	
SS		
MS		
249	the back door	
SS		
MS		
250	the front door	
SS		
MS		
251	the side door	
SS		
MS		
252	have dinner at home	
SS		
MS		

253	have dinner outside	
SS		
MS		
254	absent from	
SS		
MS		
255	like it very much	
SS		
MS		
256	unaware of	
SS		
MS		
257	a picture of	
SS		
MS		
258	look for ways to	
SS		
MS		

259	going to give	
SS		
MS		
260	going to offer	
SS		
MS		
261	something soft	
SS		
MS		
262	something hard	
SS		
MS		
263	something interesting	
SS		
MS		
264	something shocking	
SS		
MS		

265	excluded from	
SS		
MS		
266	in the juice	
SS		
MS		
267	in the fridge	
SS		
MS		
268	in the kitchen	
SS		
MS		
269	in the bowl	
SS		
MS		
270	shouted to	
SS		
MS		

271	please bring me some	
SS		
MS		
272	asked X to bring me	
SS		
MS		
273	said very loudly	
SS		
MS		
274	said to myself	
SS		
MS		
275	have a picnic	
SS		
MS		
276	left home at	
SS		
MS		

277	is afraid of	
SS		
MS		
278	talked quietly	
SS		
MS		
279	talked loudly	
SS		
MS		
280	talked with	
SS		
MS		
281	talked about	
SS		
MS		
282	talked to	
SS		
MS		

283	live near a park	
SS		
MS		
284	live close to	
SS		
MS		
285	is quite good	
SS		
MS		
286	is quite bad	
SS		
MS		
287	is not so bad	
SS		
MS		
288	is not so good	
SS		
MS		

289	is not so well	
SS		
MS		
290	soon after	
SS		
MS		
291	looking forward to	
SS		
MS		
292	walk out of	
SS		
MS		
293	not good for	
SS		
MS		
294	water down	
SS		
MS		

295	very helpful to	
SS		
MS		
296	cleaned the table	
SS		
MS		
297	washed the clothes	
SS		
MS		
298	wiped the table	
SS		
MS		
299	bought groceries at	
SS		
MS		
300	bought clothing at	
SS		
MS		

301	nobody will go	
SS		
MS		
302	nobody is coming to	
SS		
MS		
303	nobody is excited about	
SS		
MS		
304	nobody is worried about	
SS		
MS		
305	how much is it to	
SS		
MS		
306	how much does it cost to	
SS		
MS		

307	under the table	
SS		
MS		
308	found something wrong with	
SS		
MS		
309	did not find anything wrong with	
SS		
MS		
310	remains an open question	
SS		
MS		
311	until recently	
SS		
MS		
312	said hello to	
SS		
MS		

313	is dusty	
SS		
MS		
314	is smooth	
SS		
MS		
315	is rough	
SS		
MS		
316	in the street	
SS		
MS		
317	in the alley	
SS		
MS		
318	did not take	
SS		
MS		

319	shouted after	
SS		
MS		
320	doing remarkably well	
SS		
MS		
321	pulled at	
SS		
MS		
322	talked for	
SS		
MS		
323	talked at length about	
SS		
MS		
324	was surprised	
SS		
MS		

325	drove around for	
SS		
MS		
326	walked around in my slippers	
SS		
MS		
327	had a lot of toys	
SS		
MS		
328	had a lot of free time	
SS		
MS		
329	sitting at a table	
SS		
MS		
330	asked a question	
SS		
MS		

331	turned round	
SS		
MS		
332	going to visit	
SS		
MS		
333	coming to visit	
SS		
MS		
334	very seldom go to	
SS		
MS		
335	during the rain	
SS		
MS		
336	during the exam	
SS		
MS		

337	during the speech	
SS		
MS		
338	during the musical recital	
SS		
MS		
339	during the ballet performance	
SS		
MS		
340	during the soccer match	
SS		
MS		
341	said to my friend	
SS		
MS		
342	said to my teacher	
SS		
MS		

343	go for a walk	
SS		
MS		
344	walked the dog	
SS		
MS		
345	look under	
SS		
MS		
346	look above	
SS		
MS		
347	look on top of	
SS		
MS		
348	look inside	
SS		
MS		

349	have been thinking about	
SS		
MS		
350	thought about	
SS		
MS		
351	doing nothing right now	
SS		
MS		
352	it rains a lot in	
SS		
MS		
353	came back from	
SS		
MS		
354	came to	
SS		
MS		

355	every school	
SS		
MS		
356	every student	
SS		
MS		
357	every teacher	
SS		
MS		
358	a careful person	
SS		
MS		
359	a careless person	
SS		
MS		
360	take a minute to	
SS		
MS		

361	borrowed X from	
SS		
MS		
362	didn't work out	
SS		
MS		
363	when I see	
SS		
MS		
364	if I see	
SS		
MS		
365	an enjoyable evening	
SS		
MS		
366	a pleasant afternoon	
SS		
MS		

367	at the helm	
SS		
MS		
368	an entertaining performance	
SS		
MS		
369	an amusing story	
SS		
MS		
370	needs precise measurement	
SS		
MS		
371	checked X carefully	
SS		
MS		
372	costly furniture	
SS		
MS		

373	high-priced fur coat	
SS		
MS		
374	a priceless vase	
SS		
MS		
375	pricey shoes	
SS		
MS		
376	reasonably-priced	
SS		
MS		
377	at a discounted price	
SS		
MS		
378	delighted to	
SS		
MS		

379	grateful for	
SS		
MS		
380	thankful to X for	
SS		
MS		
381	thrilled to	
SS		
MS		
382	an old-fashioned kimono	
SS		
MS		
383	an age-old story	
SS		
MS		
384	giggled at	
SS		
MS		

385	sing songs	
SS		
MS		
386	paint pictures	
SS		
MS		
387	lavish praise on	
SS		
MS		
388	carrying a load	
SS		
MS		
389	carry a heavy load	
SS		
MS		
390	heavy traffic	
SS		
MS		

391	a heavy meal	
SS		
MS		
392	feel sluggish	
SS		
MS		
393	a demanding teacher	
SS		
MS		
394	posted by	
SS		
MS		
395	there's no need for	
SS		
MS		
396	brush off	
SS		
MS		

397	not surprised	
SS		
MS		
398	stick around	
SS		
MS		
399	of paramount importance	
SS		
MS		
400	without regard to	
SS		
MS		
401	there's no necessity for	
SS		
MS		
402	for a variety of reasons	
SS		
MS		

403	got a warning about	
SS		
MS		
404	got a dire warning about	
SS		
MS		
405	cooperate with	
SS		
MS		
406	named after X	
SS		
MS		
407	shoo X away	
SS		
MS		
408	totally saddened by	
SS		
MS		

409	first foray into	
SS		
MS		
410	not illegal	
SS		
MS		
411	is very unhappy about	
SS		
MS		
412	desperate to	
SS		
MS		
413	asked for information	
SS		
MS		
414	look forward to hearing	
SS		
MS		

415	not in a position to	
SS		
MS		
416	pay attention	
SS		
MS		
417	ignore the warning	
SS		
MS		
418	flat broke	
SS		
MS		
419	said very clearly	
SS		
MS		
420	began to realize that	
SS		
MS		

421	looking into	
SS		
MS		
422	forgot about	
SS		
MS		
423	warn of	
SS		
MS		
424	not a threat to	
SS		
MS		
425	expressed interest in	
SS		
MS		
426	afford the freedom to	
SS		
MS		

427	need details about	
SS		
MS		
428	stressed that there is	
SS		
MS		
429	attention to detail	
SS		
MS		
430	seem to	
SS		
MS		
431	chat with	
SS		
MS		
432	is/was believed to	
SS		
MS		

433	whether to	
SS		
MS		
434	doesn't always have to be	
SS		
MS		
435	there's plenty of hope for	
SS		
MS		
436	an attempt to	
SS		
MS		
437	a readiness to	
SS		
MS		
438	get a moment's peace from	
SS		
MS		

439	equally happy to	
SS		
MS		
440	love to see	
SS		
MS		
441	fine by me	
SS		
MS		
442	won't need to	
SS		
MS		
443	bombarded with	
SS		
MS		
444	a major misunderstanding between A and B	
SS		
MS		

445	inquiries about	
SS		
MS		
446	is/was a frenzy of interest in	
SS		
MS		
447	famous for	
SS		
MS		
448	forced to	
SS		
MS		
449	not recruiting	
SS		
MS		
450	face a shortage of	
SS		
MS		

451	no mention of	
SS		
MS		
452	a failed attempt	
SS		
MS		
453	convicted of	
SS		
MS		
454	no matter what	
SS		
MS		
455	obliged to	
SS		
MS		
456	a major issue	
SS		
MS		

457	except when	
SS		
MS		
458	stand around	
SS		
MS		
459	a proper conversation	
SS		
MS		
460	sneak a look at	
SS		
MS		
461	monopolized by	
SS		
MS		
462	less addicted to	
SS		
MS		

463	lured back to	
SS		
MS		
464	tried unsuccessfully to	
SS		
MS		
465	led to the capture of	
SS		
MS		
466	lived peacefully in	
SS		
MS		
467	pointed the finger at	
SS		
MS		
468	in deep financial trouble	
SS		
MS		

469	despite efforts by X	
SS		
MS		
470	did not respond to	
SS		
MS		
471	freaked out	
SS		
MS		
472	flew under the radar	
SS		
MS		
473	play a major role in	
SS		
MS		
474	worked to identify	
SS		
MS		

475	pleaded not guilty to	
SS		
MS		
476	does not end when	
SS		
MS		
477	contact anyone back home	
SS		
MS		
478	can be jarring	
SS		
MS		
479	a recent increase in	
SS		
MS		
480	over a span of	
SS		
MS		

481	made a total of	
SS		
MS		
482	not by accident	
SS		
MS		
483	relatively old	
SS		
MS		
484	a phalanx of television cameras	
SS		
MS		
485	circling around	
SS		
MS		
486	not that bad	
SS		
MS		

487	is a place for people to	
SS		
MS		
488	a word of warning	
SS		
MS		
489	spending some time	
SS		
MS		
490	hunger for	
SS		
MS		
491	trying to compare	
SS		
MS		
492	don't recommend	
SS		
MS		

493	sitting around	
SS		
MS		
494	no one believed	
SS		
MS		
495	in order to be	
SS		
MS		
496	didn't realize how	
SS		
MS		
497	walking down the street	
SS		
MS		
498	how often	
SS		
MS		

499	made it possible	
SS		
MS		
500	come forward	
SS		
MS		
501	can do both	
SS		
MS		
502	it takes a remarkable person to	
SS		
MS		
503	different options	
SS		
MS		
504	making an effort to	
SS		
MS		

505	one of the best things	
SS		
MS		
506	treat people badly	
SS		
MS		
507	treat people well	
SS		
MS		
508	regardless of	
SS		
MS		
509	need to watch	
SS		
MS		
510	not that good	
SS		
MS		

511	so far from	
SS		
MS		
512	so far to go	
SS		
MS		
513	unsure of	
SS		
MS		
514	have to think about	
SS		
MS		
515	terrified of	
SS		
MS		
516	safe in	
SS		
MS		

517	it was awesome	
SS		
MS		
518	there is nothing wrong with	
SS		
MS		
519	in a different way	
SS		
MS		
520	before we got to	
SS		
MS		
521	not really impressed by	
SS		
MS		
522	still talking about	
SS		
MS		

523	used as	
SS		
MS		
524	is nothing new	
SS		
MS		
525	pretended that	
SS		
MS		
526	as long as I've known	
SS		
MS		
527	foolish behaviour	
SS		
MS		
528	a little bit of	
SS		
MS		

529	not so healthy	
SS		
MS		
530	it does not take a lot to	
SS		
MS		
531	pulled in so many different directions	
SS		
MS		
532	an opportunity to try	
SS		
MS		
533	part of the problem with	
SS		
MS		
534	a finicky eater	
SS		
MS		

535	inspired me	
SS		
MS		
536	find ways to	
SS		
MS		
537	finding new ways to	
SS		
MS		
538	a lot less	
SS		
MS		
539	enjoy the finer things in life	
SS		
MS		
540	not for long	
SS		
MS		

541	when you started	
SS		
MS		
542	not as easy as	
SS		
MS		
543	not stressful	
SS		
MS		
544	the goal was to	
SS		
MS		
545	in (one's) travels	
SS		
MS		
546	influence of	
SS		
MS		

547	one of the greatest things	
SS		
MS		
548	was unbelievable	
SS		
MS		
549	always going to	
SS		
MS		
550	harsh critic	
SS		
MS		
551	on special occasions	
SS		
MS		
552	more interested in	
SS		
MS		

553	it came down to	
SS		
MS		
554	didn't start in	
SS		
MS		
555	let loose	
SS		
MS		
556	go-to food	
SS		
MS		
557	must end	
SS		
MS		
558	fly a lot	
SS		
MS		

559	not as picky as	
SS		
MS		
560	incredible skills	
SS		
MS		
561	cook with	
SS		
MS		
562	do (something) on the fly	
SS		
MS		
563	in a bind	
SS		
MS		
564	never goes bad	
SS		
MS		

565	made with	
SS		
MS		
566	makes life easier	
SS		
MS		
567	the trick to	
SS		
MS		
568	play a vital role	
SS		
MS		
569	far outlasts	
SS		
MS		
570	also hope	
SS		
MS		

571	just wondering	
SS		
MS		
572	on either side of	
SS		
MS		
573	has a peculiar background	
SS		
MS		
574	made clear to me	
SS		
MS		
575	on the edge	
SS		
MS		
576	very harsh	
SS		
MS		

577	left behind	
SS		
MS		
578	became interested in	
SS		
MS		
579	traffic was so bad	
SS		
MS		
580	don't know how to	
SS		
MS		
581	there's something beautiful about	
SS		
MS		
582	need to listen to	
SS		
MS		

583	spending weeks with	
SS		
MS		
584	come across	
SS		
MS		
585	the bizarreness of	
SS		
MS		
586	listened delightfully to	
SS		
MS		
587	not so nice	
SS		
MS		
588	never got performed	
SS		
MS		

589	a brilliant person	
SS		
MS		
590	let off steam	
SS		
MS		
591	took the decision to	
SS		
MS		
592	has the latitude to	
SS		
MS		
593	lavish attention on	
SS		
MS		
594	win praise for	
SS		
MS		

595	lose sight of	
SS		
MS		
596	all kinds of barriers	
SS		
MS		
597	tend to focus on	
SS		
MS		
598	burned to the ground	
SS		
MS		
599	bright, beautiful day	
SS		
MS		
600	hurried home	
SS		
MS		

601	was disgusted by	
SS		
MS		
602	it was as though	
SS		
MS		
603	appetite was sated	
SS		
MS		
604	daily chores	
SS		
MS		
605	dread of	
SS		
MS		
606	from time to time	
SS		
MS		

607	in moments of crisis	
SS		
MS		
608	the self-destruction of	
SS		
MS		
609	constantly at war	
SS		
MS		
610	couldn't help but	
SS		
MS		
611	can see some parallels between A and B	
SS		
MS		
612	set into motion at	
SS		
MS		

613	set in motion by	
SS		
MS		
614	the most powerful organization	
SS		
MS		
615	unable to deal with	
SS		
MS		
616	never been so anxious	
SS		
MS		
617	no one knows how to	
SS		
MS		
618	in support of	
SS		
MS		

619	take advantage of	
SS		
MS		
620	can't wrap (one's) head around	
SS		
MS		
621	deepen understanding of	
SS		
MS		
622	terribly boring	
SS		
MS		
623	does not matter that much	
SS		
MS		
624	a funny experience	
SS		
MS		

625	is/was exposed to	
SS		
MS		
626	if you listen long enough	
SS		
MS		
627	a hopeful story	
SS		
MS		
628	look back upon history	
SS		
MS		
629	free to be	
SS		
MS		
630	so anxious about	
SS		
MS		

631	all the time	
SS		
MS		
632	not a surprise	
SS		
MS		
633	ability to juggle	
SS		
MS		
634	enraged by	
SS		
MS		
635	greatly influential	
SS		
MS		
636	make fun of	
SS		
MS		

637	bare room	
SS		
MS		
638	bumped into	
SS		
MS		
639	had been cut	
SS		
MS		
640	successfully concluded	
SS		
MS		
641	sounded like	
SS		
MS		
642	the city at night	
SS		
MS		

643	fight fire with fire	
SS		
MS		
644	invaded by	
SS		
MS		
645	read aloud	
SS		
MS		
646	become contagious	
SS		
MS		
647	scratched away	
SS		
MS		
648	make the cut	
SS		
MS		

649	already crowded	
SS		
MS		
650	the beginning of	
SS		
MS		
651	whispered to	
SS		
MS		
652	appear before (someone)	
SS		
MS		
653	full coverage of	
SS		
MS		
654	an associate of	
SS		
MS		

655	highly confident that	
SS		
MS		
656	might be interested in	
SS		
MS		
657	certainly acknowledge that	
SS		
MS		
658	far more than	
SS		
MS		
659	hid behind	
SS		
MS		
660	a place of dreams	
SS		
MS		

661	moving very quickly	
SS		
MS		
662	paint a grim picture of	
SS		
MS		
663	living up to	
SS		
MS		
664	not living up to	
SS		
MS		
665	on the corner	
SS		
MS		
666	in the corner	
SS		
MS		

667	propped against	
SS		
MS		
668	command the attention of	
SS		
MS		
669	make inroads into	
SS		
MS		
670	has a pretty good track record	
SS		
MS		
671	a last-ditch effort	
SS		
MS		
672	at odds with	
SS		
MS		

673	get tough on	
SS		
MS		
674	real quick	
SS		
MS		
675	look for signs of	
SS		
MS		
676	lose faith in	
SS		
MS		
677	sending mixed messages	
SS		
MS		
678	give X the green light	
SS		
MS		

679	have a field day with	
SS		
MS		
680	start from the top	
SS		
MS		
681	all or nothing	
SS		
MS		
682	beginning to see what	
SS		
MS		
683	in the process	
SS		
MS		
684	rewarded with	
SS		
MS		

685	a remarkable achievement	
SS		
MS		
686	can be a step towards	
SS		
MS		
687	while accepting that	
SS		
MS		
688	it would be hard to imagine	
SS		
MS		
689	less than a year	
SS		
MS		
690	a vision of	
SS		
MS		

691	speak softly	
SS		
MS		
692	at dawn	
SS		
MS		
693	learn the history of	
SS		
MS		
694	doesn't entirely square with	
SS		
MS		
695	gestured at	
SS		
MS		
696	once said that	
SS		
MS		

697	it is not for	
SS		
MS		
698	work twice as hard	
SS		
MS		
699	took a long time to	
SS		
MS		
700	in theory…in practice	
SS		
MS		
701	a volcanic temper	
SS		
MS		
702	extremely poor judgment	
SS		
MS		

703	a bizarre spectacle	
SS		
MS		
704	dealing with	
SS		
MS		
705	it doesn't sound as if	
SS		
MS		
706	what gets me really excited	
SS		
MS		
707	feel a need for	
SS		
MS		
708	everyday items	
SS		
MS		

709	it's very important to	
SS		
MS		
710	angry at	
SS		
MS		
711	need extra room	
SS		
MS		
712	make a living	
SS		
MS		
713	strength and endurance	
SS		
MS		
714	what's really important is	
SS		
MS		

715	in a strange way	
SS		
MS		
716	become agitated	
SS		
MS		
717	very soothing	
SS		
MS		
718	often start doing	
SS		
MS		
719	lower (one's) anxiety	
SS		
MS		
720	really suspect	
SS		
MS		

721	strongly believe that	
SS		
MS		
722	having a bad day	
SS		
MS		
723	a big family	
SS		
MS		
724	is laughable	
SS		
MS		
725	told off	
SS		
MS		
726	the perfect dream	
SS		
MS		

727	get really nervous	
SS		
MS		
728	no one cares about	
SS		
MS		
729	no one cares for	
SS		
MS		
730	blames X on	
SS		
MS		
731	do something different	
SS		
MS		
732	perfectly unbelievable	
SS		
MS		

733	worthy of	
SS		
MS		
734	look much further	
SS		
MS		
735	walk away from	
SS		
MS		
736	waiting for an opportunity	
SS		
MS		
737	felt such pain	
SS		
MS		
738	there's no place for	
SS		
MS		

739	differ from	
SS		
MS		
740	without doubt	
SS		
MS		
741	come into effect	
SS		
MS		
742	line of thinking	
SS		
MS		
743	due to	
SS		
MS		
744	distinguish between	
SS		
MS		

745	inferior product	
SS		
MS		
746	math formula	
SS		
MS		
747	infant formula	
SS		
MS		
748	listening in rapt attention	
SS		
MS		
749	a pile of clothes	
SS		
MS		
750	a piece of machinery	
SS		
MS		

751	come from humble beginnings	
SS		
MS		
752	full of energy	
SS		
MS		
753	carefully observe	
SS		
MS		
754	a council of experts	
SS		
MS		
755	fit for	
SS		
MS		
756	on guard	
SS		
MS		

757	work with whomever	
SS		
MS		
758	what counts most	
SS		
MS		
759	have a duty to	
SS		
MS		
760	one of the most vexing problems	
SS		
MS		
761	informed debate	
SS		
MS		
762	take some pleasure in	
SS		
MS		

763	biggest concern is	
SS		
MS		
764	incredibly timely	
SS		
MS		
765	want to point out that	
SS		
MS		
766	will benefit from knowing that	
SS		
MS		
767	feel free to	
SS		
MS		
768	get the show on the road	
SS		
MS		

769	do almost nothing to	
SS		
MS		
770	superbly qualified	
SS		
MS		
771	renowned as	
SS		
MS		
772	point a way forward	
SS		
MS		
773	cut deals worth	
SS		
MS		
774	cultivate a stable of	
SS		
MS		

775	resolved to	
SS		
MS		
776	ride the wave of	
SS		
MS		
777	the real turning point	
SS		
MS		
778	evolve into	
SS		
MS		
779	what it means to	
SS		
MS		
780	quite savvy	
SS		
MS		

781	what is needed to	
SS		
MS		
782	take a cut of	
SS		
MS		
783	an unsettling call	
SS		
MS		
784	more engaged than	
SS		
MS		
785	hefty fees	
SS		
MS		
786	conducive to	
SS		
MS		

787	have the inside track on	
SS		
MS		
788	in tune with	
SS		
MS		
789	set a tone of	
SS		
MS		
790	play it safe	
SS		
MS		
791	in the trenches	
SS		
MS		
792	shape the understanding of	
SS		
MS		

793	mimicked by	
SS		
MS		
794	take off	
SS		
MS		
795	fast forward to	
SS		
MS		
796	a little rusty	
SS		
MS		
797	jot down	
SS		
MS		
798	omit from	
SS		
MS		

799	not going to sugarcoat	
SS		
MS		
800	produced in	
SS		
MS		
801	born in	
SS		
MS		
802	the most influential leader	
SS		
MS		
803	an advisor on	
SS		
MS		
804	helped make possible	
SS		
MS		

805	waiting for confirmation	
SS		
MS		
806	gone far	
SS		
MS		
807	constantly surprised	
SS		
MS		
808	permanently preserved	
SS		
MS		
809	on the same date	
SS		
MS		
810	no attempt at	
SS		
MS		

811	while waiting for	
SS		
MS		
812	without the assistance of	
SS		
MS		
813	not quite sure	
SS		
MS		
814	discouraging surroundings	
SS		
MS		
815	as compared with	
SS		
MS		
816	whispered conversations	
SS		
MS		

817	there is a reason why	
SS		
MS		
818	conveyed from X to Y	
SS		
MS		
819	in the days of	
SS		
MS		
820	know even less	
SS		
MS		
821	take an interest in	
SS		
MS		
822	also used for	
SS		
MS		

823	unusual nature of	
SS		
MS		
824	in addition to	
SS		
MS		
825	come under fire for	
SS		
MS		
826	at will	
SS		
MS		
827	could not understand the necessity of	
SS		
MS		
828	scared for	
SS		
MS		

829	open for discussion	
SS		
MS		
830	trying to underscore	
SS		
MS		
831	wondering about	
SS		
MS		
832	a glimpse into	
SS		
MS		
833	on a working vacation	
SS		
MS		
834	only recently come to light	
SS		
MS		

835	did have advance knowledge	
SS		
MS		
836	nothing has changed about	
SS		
MS		
837	have concern for	
SS		
MS		
838	very close to	
SS		
MS		
839	potential effect on	
SS		
MS		
840	should not be close	
SS		
MS		

841	an unexpected guest	
SS		
MS		
842	a prime example of	
SS		
MS		
843	certainly could be	
SS		
MS		
844	has been moving quite quickly	
SS		
MS		
845	stop meddling in	
SS		
MS		
846	rescued from	
SS		
MS		

847	hold a meeting	
SS		
MS		
848	jeer at	
SS		
MS		
849	try to save	
SS		
MS		
850	refuse to concede	
SS		
MS		
851	donated money	
SS		
MS		
852	pled guilty	
SS		
MS		

853	no verifiable way to	
SS		
MS		
854	is too early to tell	
SS		
MS		
855	send a powerful message	
SS		
MS		
856	head of	
SS		
MS		
857	at the very top	
SS		
MS		
858	on Twitter	
SS		
MS		

859	caused damage to	
SS		
MS		
860	in the summer of	
SS		
MS		
861	a makeshift compound	
SS		
MS		
862	headed towards	
SS		
MS		
863	has no clue	
SS		
MS		
864	faced off with	
SS		
MS		

865	dispersed the crowds	
SS		
MS		
866	dozens of buildings	
SS		
MS		
867	hurricane season	
SS		
MS		
868	take aim at	
SS		
MS		
869	a rare occurrence	
SS		
MS		
870	not a rare occurrence	
SS		
MS		

871	for the purpose of	
SS		
MS		
872	in the playground	
SS		
MS		
873	contrasts with	
SS		
MS		
874	in that direction	
SS		
MS		
875	for the next several days	
SS		
MS		
876	it is hard to gauge	
SS		
MS		

877	know within a short time	
SS		
MS		
878	at least until	
SS		
MS		
879	one piece of news	
SS		
MS		
880	hear directly from	
SS		
MS		
881	sources tell X that	
SS		
MS		
882	has reason to worry about	
SS		
MS		

883	the most urgent problem	
SS		
MS		
884	will happen before	
SS		
MS		
885	about to leave	
SS		
MS		
886	a guilty verdict	
SS		
MS		
887	a smear on	
SS		
MS		
888	don't want to admit	
SS		
MS		

889	en route to	
SS		
MS		
890	neck and neck	
SS		
MS		
891	a precursor to	
SS		
MS		
892	a tough race	
SS		
MS		
893	want to have change	
SS		
MS		
894	a shrewd strategy	
SS		
MS		

895	proved to be right	
SS		
MS		
896	the wrong impression	
SS		
MS		
897	in demand	
SS		
MS		
898	till it turned	
SS		
MS		
899	a wonderful new X	
SS		
MS		
900	hard to keep track of	
SS		
MS		

901	shake hands	
SS		
MS		
902	know more about	
SS		
MS		
903	receive a pension	
SS		
MS		
904	receive an allowance	
SS		
MS		
905	receive a stipend	
SS		
MS		
906	receive an honorarium	
SS		
MS		

907	honor a request for	
SS		
MS		
908	approve a request for	
SS		
MS		
909	earn a living doing	
SS		
MS		
910	have (one) nails trimmed	
SS		
MS		
911	stub (one's) toe against	
SS		
MS		
912	you had better	
SS		
MS		

913	shocked that	
SS		
MS		
914	received a helping hand	
SS		
MS		
915	fierce support	
SS		
MS		
916	has a scar	
SS		
MS		
917	at your own convenience	
SS		
MS		
918	at your earliest convenience	
SS		
MS		

919	a return ticket	
SS		
MS		
920	a round-trip ticket	
SS		
MS		
921	who is to blame for	
SS		
MS		
922	add some	
SS		
MS		
923	try long enough	
SS		
MS		
924	in the lost and found	
SS		
MS		

925	fooled by appearances	
SS		
MS		
926	made a lot of progress	
SS		
MS		
927	murdered by	
SS		
MS		
928	at the stroke of midnight	
SS		
MS		
929	accidentally exposed	
SS		
MS		
930	got X to accept	
SS		
MS		

931	it's always very difficult to	
SS		
MS		
932	get ready for	
SS		
MS		
933	a lot of property	
SS		
MS		
934	in disguise	
SS		
MS		
935	wore a disguise	
SS		
MS		
936	a blessing in disguise	
SS		
MS		

937	pretty unclear about	
SS		
MS		
938	the speed at which	
SS		
MS		
939	as long as	
SS		
MS		
940	choose between A and B	
SS		
MS		
941	convenient for	
SS		
MS		
942	gave a clear description of	
SS		
MS		

943	warm thanks to	
SS		
MS		
944	marvelous device	
SS		
MS		
945	arranged to do	
SS		
MS		
946	the width of	
SS		
MS		
947	the length of	
SS		
MS		
948	the breadth of	
SS		
MS		

949	overlooking a garden	
SS		
MS		
950	wooden shutters	
SS		
MS		
951	a damp room	
SS		
MS		
952	bread crumbs on the	
SS		
MS		
953	use a rake for	
SS		
MS		
954	use a spade to	
SS		
MS		

955	ashamed of	
SS		
MS		
956	apply for	
SS		
MS		
957	apply to	
SS		
MS		
958	in appearance	
SS		
MS		
959	speak in anger	
SS		
MS		
960	admit X to	
SS		
MS		

961	amazed at how much	
SS		
MS		
962	in advance of	
SS		
MS		
963	acts on	
SS		
MS		
964	angry because	
SS		
MS		
965	a secret passage	
SS		
MS		
966	earn a commission	
SS		
MS		

967	hum of conversation	
SS		
MS		
968	rusted nails	
SS		
MS		
969	a solemn funeral	
SS		
MS		
970	very popular	
SS		
MS		
971	take offence to	
SS		
MS		
972	intend to	
SS		
MS		

973	break ground	
SS		
MS		
974	heard many suggestions	
SS		
MS		
975	no real proof	
SS		
MS		
976	is not the issue	
SS		
MS		
977	the destruction of	
SS		
MS		
978	a terrible accident	
SS		
MS		

979	omitted from	
SS		
MS		
980	the actual amount of	
SS		
MS		
981	seem incapable of	
SS		
MS		
982	commence discussions about	
SS		
MS		
983	on the condition that	
SS		
MS		
984	show affection	
SS		
MS		

985	apart from	
SS		
MS		
986	appear weak	
SS		
MS		
987	bare knuckle	
SS		
MS		
988	brief meeting	
SS		
MS		
989	broad road	
SS		
MS		
990	calm seas	
SS		
MS		

991	capture the image	
SS		
MS		
992	a school uniform	
SS		
MS		
993	pluck some feathers	
SS		
MS		
994	a spitting image	
SS		
MS		
995	splitting logs	
SS		
MS		
996	licking its paws	
SS		
MS		

997	a barking dog	
SS		
MS		
998	scratching the ground	
SS		
MS		
999	peck at	
SS		
MS		
1,000	in the horse stable	
SS		
MS		
1,001	in the bullpen	
SS		
MS		
1,002	withered leaves	
SS		
MS		

1,003	so wild that	
SS		
MS		
1,004	long stalks of corn	
SS		
MS		
1,005	a bountiful harvest	
SS		
MS		
1,006	a good crop	
SS		
MS		
1,007	on its way to	
SS		
MS		
1,008	a load of wheat	
SS		
MS		

1,009	absolute obedience	
SS		
MS		
1,010	a patch of grass	
SS		
MS		
1,011	a few thorns	
SS		
MS		
1,012	putting down a	
SS		
MS		
1,013	booted from	
SS		
MS		
1,014	think highly of	
SS		
MS		

1,015	enjoy a stunning view	
SS		
MS		
1,016	not for the fainthearted	
SS		
MS		
1,017	in revolt against	
SS		
MS		
1,018	a little lower than expected	
SS		
MS		
1,019	cower to	
SS		
MS		
1,020	had a heated exchange with	
SS		
MS		

1,021	care deeply about	
SS		
MS		
1,022	is the exact opposite of	
SS		
MS		
1,023	hold out hope that	
SS		
MS		
1,024	what led up to	
SS		
MS		
1,025	no reason for concern	
SS		
MS		
1,026	not focused enough on	
SS		
MS		

1,027	repeatedly said	
SS		
MS		
1,028	staunch supporter	
SS		
MS		
1,029	make up for lost time	
SS		
MS		
1,030	in stark contrast	
SS		
MS		
1,031	so stunned by X that	
SS		
MS		
1,032	let go of	
SS		
MS		

1,033	a good explanation from	
SS		
MS		
1,034	picked up from	
SS		
MS		
1,035	on a wild goose chase	
SS		
MS		
1,036	a guilty plea	
SS		
MS		
1,037	the second largest	
SS		
MS		
1,038	crack jokes	
SS		
MS		

1,039	wrapped up in	
SS		
MS		
1,040	not allowed in	
SS		
MS		
1,041	telling the truth	
SS		
MS		
1,042	ensnared in	
SS		
MS		
1,043	don't have anything further to say	
SS		
MS		
1,044	don't yet see how	
SS		
MS		

1,045	the bulk of	
SS		
MS		
1,046	in the months following	
SS		
MS		
1,047	took to the streets	
SS		
MS		
1,048	pretty clear that	
SS		
MS		
1,049	cause a ripple effect	
SS		
MS		
1,050	felt a great sense of relief	
SS		
MS		

1,051	be sure to	
SS		
MS		
1,052	weigh in on	
SS		
MS		
1,053	do not believe	
SS		
MS		
1,054	straight out of	
SS		
MS		
1,055	X is to me	
SS		
MS		
1,056	is/was struggling in	
SS		
MS		

1,057	there is nothing more to	
SS		
MS		
1,058	the most complex	
SS		
MS		
1,059	is/was equal to	
SS		
MS		
1,060	is/was fashionably late	
SS		
MS		
1,061	is/was all about	
SS		
MS		
1,062	saw the scene unfold	
SS		
MS		

1,063	finally got to	
SS		
MS		
1,064	get into an argument	
SS		
MS		
1,065	slightly off	
SS		
MS		
1,066	far beyond	
SS		
MS		
1,067	doubled in the last few months	
SS		
MS		
1,068	an uptick in the number of	
SS		
MS		

1,069	a little bit of both	
SS		
MS		
1,070	giving (something) out for free	
SS		
MS		
1,071	it is estimated that	
SS		
MS		
1,072	a distant dream	
SS		
MS		
1,073	had a hard time understanding	
SS		
MS		
1,074	has its place	
SS		
MS		

1,075	in suits	
SS		
MS		
1,076	on the road	
SS		
MS		
1,077	by choice	
SS		
MS		
1,078	among the attendees	
SS		
MS		
1,079	out of work	
SS		
MS		
1,080	warm up the	
SS		
MS		

1,081	go for a walk	
SS		
MS		
1,082	needn't come	
SS		
MS		
1,083	needn't do	
SS		
MS		
1,084	in use	
SS		
MS		
1,085	must be	
SS		
MS		
1,086	turn away	
SS		
MS		

1,087	agree to allow	
SS		
MS		
1,088	a recent query	
SS		
MS		
1,089	write in ink	
SS		
MS		
1,090	a different approach	
SS		
MS		
1,091	went ashore	
SS		
MS		
1,092	went aboard	
SS		
MS		

1,093	shake hands	
SS		
MS		
1,094	hold hands	
SS		
MS		
1,095	a gold medal	
SS		
MS		
1,096	a silver cup	
SS		
MS		
1,097	a wedding band	
SS		
MS		
1,098	X advised me to	
SS		
MS		

1,099	the best outcome is	
SS		
MS		
1,100	open for business	
SS		
MS		
1,101	the leading producer	
SS		
MS		
1,102	from the very beginning	
SS		
MS		
1,103	camped by	
SS		
MS		
1,104	next meeting	
SS		
MS		

1,105	did not matter	
SS		
MS		
1,106	wrote various reports	
SS		
MS		
1,107	feel sorry	
SS		
MS		
1,108	thanks for	
SS		
MS		
1,109	tie up the	
SS		
MS		
1,110	throw out	
SS		
MS		

1,111	start for home	
SS		
MS		
1,112	ran away	
SS		
MS		
1,113	run away	
SS		
MS		
1,114	put on some slippers	
SS		
MS		
1,115	sat at the dinner table	
SS		
MS		
1,116	send for	
SS		
MS		

1,117	a week before	
SS		
MS		
1,118	sell for	
SS		
MS		
1,119	the place where	
SS		
MS		
1,120	the tract that I was telling you about	
SS		
MS		
1,121	with pleasure	
SS		
MS		
1,122	I wonder whose umbrella	
SS		
MS		

1,123	walk away from	
SS		
MS		
1,124	have a warning for (someone)	
SS		
MS		
1,125	issue a warning to	
SS		
MS		
1,126	by coincidence	
SS		
MS		
1,127	the lady who lent me	
SS		
MS		
1,128	with ties to	
SS		
MS		

1,129	doesn't go	
SS		
MS		
1,130	can hardly see	
SS		
MS		
1,131	reckless behaviour	
SS		
MS		
1,132	a coal mine	
SS		
MS		
1,133	types of vegetables	
SS		
MS		
1,134	spent very little money on	
SS		
MS		

1,135	renege on	
SS		
MS		
1,136	in less than	
SS		
MS		
1,137	very close together	
SS		
MS		
1,138	extinguished the fire	
SS		
MS		
1,139	put some kindling on	
SS		
MS		
1,140	embers are going out	
SS		
MS		

1,141	take a listen to	
SS		
MS		
1,142	put up with	
SS		
MS		
1,143	as fast as	
SS		
MS		
1,144	be patient	
SS		
MS		
1,145	should not forget to	
SS		
MS		
1,146	always welcome in	
SS		
MS		

1,147	without question	
SS		
MS		
1,148	especially delighted	
SS		
MS		
1,149	make life easier	
SS		
MS		
1,150	surprised by the	
SS		
MS		
1,151	succeeded in	
SS		
MS		
1,152	always welcome	
SS		
MS		

1,153	unusual style	
SS		
MS		
1,154	photographed some	
SS		
MS		
1,155	being very careful with	
SS		
MS		
1,156	the paediatric hospital	
SS		
MS		
1,157	went to the dentist	
SS		
MS		
1,158	took pity on X	
SS		
MS		

1,159	owe X to Y	
SS		
MS		
1,160	cannot see	
SS		
MS		
1,161	make X into Y	
SS		
MS		
1,162	look after	
SS		
MS		
1,163	lock up the	
SS		
MS		
1,164	in love with	
SS		
MS		

1,165	it's the beginning of	
SS		
MS		
1,166	during my studies	
SS		
MS		
1,167	while I was studying	
SS		
MS		
1,168	during my meal	
SS		
MS		
1,169	while I was eating	
SS		
MS		
1,170	something I prize dearly is	
SS		
MS		

1,171	around the world	
SS		
MS		
1,172	walked through	
SS		
MS		
1,173	lose heart	
SS		
MS		
1,174	lose (one's) temper	
SS		
MS		
1,175	my classmates are	
SS		
MS		
1,176	cook yourself a	
SS		
MS		

1,177	there is such a tendency to	
SS		
MS		
1,178	wake (someone) up	
SS		
MS		
1,179	too strict	
SS		
MS		
1,180	a pleasant piano teacher	
SS		
MS		
1,181	a passionate teacher	
SS		
MS		
1,182	an exemplary student	
SS		
MS		

1,183	an attentive listener	
SS		
MS		
1,184	a good speaker	
SS		
MS		
1,185	deviate from	
SS		
MS		
1,186	joined the club	
SS		
MS		
1,187	latest invention	
SS		
MS		
1,188	has invented	
SS		
MS		

1,189	a stack of	
SS		
MS		
1,190	a pile of	
SS		
MS		
1,191	a piece of string	
SS		
MS		
1,192	tying a piece of	
SS		
MS		
1,193	fly a kite	
SS		
MS		
1,194	set up camp	
SS		
MS		

1,195	hold on	
SS		
MS		
1,196	hold to the	
SS		
MS		
1,197	by heart	
SS		
MS		
1,198	hear from	
SS		
MS		
1,199	got the answer right	
SS		
MS		
1,200	got the answer wrong	
SS		
MS		

1,201	too stubborn	
SS		
MS		
1,202	too large	
SS		
MS		
1,203	too small	
SS		
MS		
1,204	really classy	
SS		
MS		
1,205	really lazy	
SS		
MS		
1,206	really careless	
SS		
MS		

1,207	a complete fiasco	
SS		
MS		
1,208	travel abroad	
SS		
MS		
1,209	has bad manners	
SS		
MS		
1,210	eat a lot of	
SS		
MS		
1,211	an epic voyage	
SS		
MS		
1,212	a long journey	
SS		
MS		

1,213	always remembered to	
SS		
MS		
1,214	seem pertinent to	
SS		
MS		
1,215	expect from	
SS		
MS		
1,216	very bright	
SS		
MS		
1,217	free on the weekend	
SS		
MS		
1,218	not ready	
SS		
MS		

1,219	an encouraging sign	
SS		
MS		
1,220	has fallen asleep	
SS		
MS		
1,221	soaped the dishes	
SS		
MS		
1,222	stepped on	
SS		
MS		
1,223	a bunch of bananas	
SS		
MS		
1,224	feed the cat	
SS		
MS		

1,225	an empty bowl	
SS		
MS		
1,226	lost a wallet	
SS		
MS		
1,227	lost a wheel	
SS		
MS		
1,228	lost a tooth	
SS		
MS		
1,229	addicted to	
SS		
MS		
1,230	there has been an accident	
SS		
MS		

1,231	give food to	
SS		
MS		
1,232	feed on	
SS		
MS		
1,233	unless we do	
SS		
MS		
1,234	unless you are	
SS		
MS		
1,235	unless you do something	
SS		
MS		
1,236	got together with	
SS		
MS		

1,237	rub shoulders with	
SS		
MS		
1,238	keep company with	
SS		
MS		
1,239	a jumble of	
SS		
MS		
1,240	mingled with	
SS		
MS		
1,241	blend a number of	
SS		
MS		
1,242	mix several colours	
SS		
MS		

1,243	clear goals for	
SS		
MS		
1,244	a mysterious piece of	
SS		
MS		
1,245	weird behaviour	
SS		
MS		
1,246	abnormal posture	
SS		
MS		
1,247	otherworldly landscape	
SS		
MS		
1,248	have an uncanny resemblance to	
SS		
MS		

1,249	an eerie photograph	
SS		
MS		
1,250	melted cheese	
SS		
MS		
1,251	come to grips with	
SS		
MS		
1,252	love sailing	
SS		
MS		
1,253	in search of	
SS		
MS		
1,254	wander the streets	
SS		
MS		

1,255	people you don't know	
SS		
MS		
1,256	dusty furniture	
SS		
MS		
1,257	voiced concern over	
SS		
MS		
1,258	have a try at	
SS		
MS		
1,259	have a go at	
SS		
MS		
1,260	address a letter	
SS		
MS		

1,261	hammer a nail	
SS		
MS		
1,262	like to fish	
SS		
MS		
1,263	like to go fishing	
SS		
MS		
1,264	do (one's) own	
SS		
MS		
1,265	print a letterhead	
SS		
MS		
1,266	a huge concern	
SS		
MS		

1,267	start getting real	
SS		
MS		
1,268	followed by	
SS		
MS		
1,269	straight ahead	
SS		
MS		
1,270	a line of traffic	
SS		
MS		
1,271	an advertisement for	
SS		
MS		
1,272	smell a rat	
SS		
MS		

1,273	slip (one's) mind	
SS		
MS		
1,274	sit tight	
SS		
MS		
1,275	sit on the fence	
SS		
MS		
1,276	sleeping rough	
SS		
MS		
1,277	a rough ride	
SS		
MS		
1,278	a shallow port	
SS		
MS		

1,279	a breakthrough	
SS		
MS		
1,280	kicked into full gear	
SS		
MS		
1,281	there are some bulbs	
SS		
MS		
1,282	there are some stars	
SS		
MS		
1,283	encourage X to	
SS		
MS		
1,284	in the sky	
SS		
MS		

1,285	an island	
SS		
MS		
1,286	picture of a	
SS		
MS		
1,287	don't care much about	
SS		
MS		
1,288	absent from	
SS		
MS		
1,289	everyone came except X	
SS		
MS		
1,290	out of respect	
SS		
MS		

1,291	gone already	
SS		
MS		
1,292	gone now	
SS		
MS		
1,293	enjoy yourself	
SS		
MS		
1,294	only have	
SS		
MS		
1,295	in a few minutes	
SS		
MS		
1,296	forgot to bring	
SS		
MS		

1,297	was born in	
SS		
MS		
1,298	for you to sit on	
SS		
MS		
1,299	apologize to	
SS		
MS		
1,300	apologize for	
SS		
MS		
1,301	weighs about two kilograms	
SS		
MS		
1,302	weighs five pounds	
SS		
MS		

1,303	rise to the occasion	
SS		
MS		
1,304	at the post office	
SS		
MS		
1,305	mail a package	
SS		
MS		
1,306	how much does it cost to	
SS		
MS		
1,307	that way	
SS		
MS		
1,308	this way	
SS		
MS		

1,309	haven't read	
SS		
MS		
1,310	haven't seen	
SS		
MS		
1,311	what's happening	
SS		
MS		
1,312	what happened to	
SS		
MS		
1,313	the best colour for	
SS		
MS		
1,314	lay eggs	
SS		
MS		

1,315	it is true that	
SS		
MS		
1,316	it's no myth that	
SS		
MS		
1,317	in the downtown area	
SS		
MS		
1,318	in the suburbs	
SS		
MS		
1,319	at the outskirts of the city	
SS		
MS		
1,320	outside the city	
SS		
MS		

1,321	getting through the exam was	
SS		
MS		
1,322	getting through the city is	
SS		
MS		
1,323	a distance of	
SS		
MS		
1,324	filled the bucket with	
SS		
MS		
1,325	filled the cup with	
SS		
MS		
1,326	fifty kilometers is	
SS		
MS		

1,327	ten minutes is	
SS		
MS		
1,328	the whole class	
SS		
MS		
1,329	the whole family	
SS		
MS		
1,330	whichever you prefer	
SS		
MS		
1,331	going to snow	
SS		
MS		
1,332	going to rain	
SS		
MS		

1,333	defend (one's) honor	
SS		
MS		
1,334	perfectly normal lives	
SS		
MS		
1,335	it's no wonder that	
SS		
MS		
1,336	conceived in	
SS		
MS		
1,337	helpful in	
SS		
MS		
1,338	the vast majority of	
SS		
MS		

1,339	cut a deal with	
SS		
MS		
1,340	around the globe	
SS		
MS		
1,341	a clever fellow	
SS		
MS		
1,342	haven't heard any news about	
SS		
MS		
1,343	stood staring at	
SS		
MS		
1,344	break the news	
SS		
MS		

1,345	travelled with a tour group	
SS		
MS		
1,346	travelled alone	
SS		
MS		
1,347	travelled with friends	
SS		
MS		
1,348	won the race	
SS		
MS		
1,349	stepped on my foot	
SS		
MS		
1,350	slipped on	
SS		
MS		

1,351	be careful how	
SS		
MS		
1,352	be careful not to	
SS		
MS		
1,353	after the movie	
SS		
MS		
1,354	the main event started at	
SS		
MS		
1,355	told X to	
SS		
MS		
1,356	made a big mistake	
SS		
MS		

1,357	climbed up the ladder	
SS		
MS		
1,358	gave the children a test	
SS		
MS		
1,359	looked around the	
SS		
MS		
1,360	does not change	
SS		
MS		
1,361	an impregnable castle	
SS		
MS		
1,362	an impenetrable wall	
SS		
MS		

1,363	seemed indestructible	
SS		
MS		
1,364	a fit cheerleader	
SS		
MS		
1,365	a hefty bill	
SS		
MS		
1,366	a powerful leader	
SS		
MS		
1,367	a strong government	
SS		
MS		
1,368	sounded like	
SS		
MS		

1,369	a cruel attack	
SS		
MS		
1,370	mean-spirited behaviour	
SS		
MS		
1,371	filthy room	
SS		
MS		
1,372	squalid conditions	
SS		
MS		
1,373	sickening feeling	
SS		
MS		
1,374	frightful dream	
SS		
MS		

1,375	dreadful experience	
SS		
MS		
1,376	disgusting taste	
SS		
MS		
1,377	distressing news	
SS		
MS		
1,378	a shattering blow	
SS		
MS		
1,379	shattered by the news	
SS		
MS		
1,380	smash to smithereens	
SS		
MS		

1,381	break into pieces	
SS		
MS		
1,382	broken dreams	
SS		
MS		
1,383	a good night's sleep	
SS		
MS		
1,384	a lovely package	
SS		
MS		
1,385	a good soccer player	
SS		
MS		
1,386	a good tennis player	
SS		
MS		

1,387	a done deal	
SS		
MS		
1,388	an insect sting	
SS		
MS		
1,389	a dog bite	
SS		
MS		
1,390	keep my promise	
SS		
MS		
1,391	smelled something funny	
SS		
MS		
1,392	promised to be	
SS		
MS		

1,393	order me another	
SS		
MS		
1,394	order me a coffee	
SS		
MS		
1,395	have a quick look	
SS		
MS		
1,396	look outside	
SS		
MS		
1,397	look inside	
SS		
MS		
1,398	can you guess where	
SS		
MS		

1,399	eating the corn off the cob	
SS		
MS		
1,400	eating the meat off the bone	
SS		
MS		
1,401	chain the dog	
SS		
MS		
1,402	unleash the dog	
SS		
MS		
1,403	put the dog on a leash	
SS		
MS		
1,404	guess who	
SS		
MS		

1,405	trying to lower the expectations	
SS		
MS		
1,406	nearer to	
SS		
MS		
1,407	nearest the	
SS		
MS		
1,408	hopping mad	
SS		
MS		
1,409	in the tree	
SS		
MS		
1,410	mountain goats	
SS		
MS		

1,411	a square-jawed man	
SS		
MS		
1,412	high cheekbones	
SS		
MS		
1,413	a broad forehead	
SS		
MS		
1,414	a well-trimmed moustache	
SS		
MS		
1,415	a long beard	
SS		
MS		
1,416	watching the cake	
SS		
MS		

1,417	running after	
SS		
MS		
1,418	flying about	
SS		
MS		
1,419	flying above	
SS		
MS		
1,420	latch on to	
SS		
MS		
1,421	perched on a tree branch	
SS		
MS		
1,422	a butterfly	
SS		
MS		

1,423	a button	
SS		
MS		
1,424	an insecticide	
SS		
MS		
1,425	different kinds of	
SS		
MS		
1,426	to the left of	
SS		
MS		
1,427	further away	
SS		
MS		
1,428	in a cage	
SS		
MS		

1,429	on the mountain	
SS		
MS		
1,430	in a zoo	
SS		
MS		
1,431	on the green grass	
SS		
MS		
1,432	justified in	
SS		
MS		
1,433	a rubber duck	
SS		
MS		
1,434	a piece of ribbon	
SS		
MS		

1,435	the merchant	
SS		
MS		
1,436	in the magazine	
SS		
MS		
1,437	a piece of cloth	
SS		
MS		
1,438	learning to	
SS		
MS		
1,439	on pins and needles	
SS		
MS		
1,440	the crux of the problem	
SS		
MS		

1,441	is knitting	
SS		
MS		
1,442	on the left, there is	
SS		
MS		
1,443	middle of	
SS		
MS		
1,444	there's no circumstance under which	
SS		
MS		
1,445	need to work together	
SS		
MS		
1,446	even more urgent than	
SS		
MS		

1,447	very inexpensively	
SS		
MS		
1,448	a head-scratching comment	
SS		
MS		
1,449	extricate X from	
SS		
MS		
1,450	painstaking work	
SS		
MS		
1,451	entirely dependent on	
SS		
MS		
1,452	in turmoil	
SS		
MS		

1,453	work hard at	
SS		
MS		
1,454	help with access	
SS		
MS		
1,455	start a dialogue	
SS		
MS		
1,456	exit strategy	
SS		
MS		
1,457	fill the vacuum	
SS		
MS		
1,458	friendly to	
SS		
MS		

1,459	on the right path	
SS		
MS		
1,460	tested for	
SS		
MS		
1,461	feeling exhausted	
SS		
MS		
1,462	not proud of	
SS		
MS		
1,463	swore at	
SS		
MS		
1,464	the target of	
SS		
MS		

1,465	media blitz	
SS		
MS		
1,466	is all smiles	
SS		
MS		
1,467	hit back at	
SS		
MS		
1,468	which one is better	
SS		
MS		
1,469	a large blaze	
SS		
MS		
1,470	give up control of	
SS		
MS		

1,471	arrested for	
SS		
MS		
1,472	rescued from	
SS		
MS		
1,473	buried in	
SS		
MS		
1,474	stranded on	
SS		
MS		
1,475	stranded in	
SS		
MS		
1,476	adorable puppies	
SS		
MS		

1,477	testify on	
SS		
MS		
1,478	every single time	
SS		
MS		
1,479	placed on leave	
SS		
MS		
1,480	a wardrobe malfunction	
SS		
MS		
1,481	after the incident	
SS		
MS		
1,482	connect with	
SS		
MS		

1,483	bad information	
SS		
MS		
1,484	beset with rumors	
SS		
MS		
1,485	diagnosed by	
SS		
MS		
1,486	keep making it easier	
SS		
MS		
1,487	put up or shut up	
SS		
MS		
1,488	look back on	
SS		
MS		

1,489	had nothing to do with	
SS		
MS		
1,490	got paid for	
SS		
MS		
1,491	in financial trouble	
SS		
MS		
1,492	dive into	
SS		
MS		
1,493	catch (someone) off-guard	
SS		
MS		
1,494	deal with problems	
SS		
MS		

1,495	grown in leaps and bounds	
SS		
MS		
1,496	one of the most beloved	
SS		
MS		
1,497	a star-studded event	
SS		
MS		
1,498	voluntarily came forward	
SS		
MS		
1,499	came into prominence	
SS		
MS		
1,500	determine whether	
SS		
MS		

1,501	is laser-focused	
SS		
MS		
1,502	an ongoing interest in	
SS		
MS		
1,503	a reaction to	
SS		
MS		
1,504	will no doubt hear	
SS		
MS		
1,505	no matter how many times	
SS		
MS		
1,506	it should be no surprise that	
SS		
MS		

1,507	took the oath of office	
SS		
MS		
1,508	breaking records	
SS		
MS		
1,509	entangled in	
SS		
MS		
1,510	the unpleasant duty	
SS		
MS		
1,511	squeamish about	
SS		
MS		
1,512	is a warm-up for	
SS		
MS		

1,513	is a force for good	
SS		
MS		
1,514	rarely talk about	
SS		
MS		
1,515	tax cut	
SS		
MS		
1,516	crisscrossing the country	
SS		
MS		
1,517	unusual arrangement	
SS		
MS		
1,518	no one knows	
SS		
MS		

1,519	eager to	
SS		
MS		
1,520	other than	
SS		
MS		
1,521	in earnest	
SS		
MS		
1,522	substantially better than	
SS		
MS		
1,523	give up	
SS		
MS		
1,524	so much	
SS		
MS		

1,525	regard as	
SS		
MS		
1,526	decide to	
SS		
MS		
1,527	figure out	
SS		
MS		
1,528	head to	
SS		
MS		
1,529	participate in	
SS		
MS		
1,530	listen to	
SS		
MS		

1,531	squeeze in	
SS		
MS		
1,532	desire to be	
SS		
MS		
1,533	have a big impact on	
SS		
MS		
1,534	cause concern for	
SS		
MS		
1,535	forged close ties with	
SS		
MS		
1,536	just a few months ago	
SS		
MS		

1,537	for those using	
SS		
MS		
1,538	have enough evidence	
SS		
MS		
1,539	wind up	
SS		
MS		
1,540	should be concerned	
SS		
MS		
1,541	the past couple of weeks	
SS		
MS		
1,542	says too much	
SS		
MS		

1,543	at a certain point	
SS		
MS		
1,544	approved going ahead with	
SS		
MS		
1,545	in the process of	
SS		
MS		
1,546	expect to hear more about	
SS		
MS		
1,547	it is clear to see	
SS		
MS		
1,548	go after	
SS		
MS		

1,549	in serious jeopardy	
SS		
MS		
1,550	will get real bad real fast	
SS		
MS		
1,551	take a closer look	
SS		
MS		
1,552	hunkered down	
SS		
MS		
1,553	not at issue	
SS		
MS		
1,554	know in advance	
SS		
MS		

1,555	on good terms	
SS		
MS		
1,556	frustrated by	
SS		
MS		
1,557	plead guilty	
SS		
MS		
1,558	on the eve of	
SS		
MS		
1,559	in panic	
SS		
MS		
1,560	kowtow to	
SS		
MS		

1,561	muddy the waters	
SS		
MS		
1,562	eke out a living	
SS		
MS		
1,563	do nothing about	
SS		
MS		
1,564	at this moment	
SS		
MS		
1,565	it's just not	
SS		
MS		
1,566	quite as noisy as	
SS		
MS		

1,567	under consideration	
SS		
MS		
1,568	depend on	
SS		
MS		
1,569	from the very beginning	
SS		
MS		
1,570	been in place for	
SS		
MS		
1,571	nothing specific	
SS		
MS		
1,572	a rosy assessment	
SS		
MS		

1,573	trying to convince	
SS		
MS		
1,574	reassess one's views	
SS		
MS		
1,575	very gracious	
SS		
MS		
1,576	much bigger than	
SS		
MS		
1,577	essential to the survival of	
SS		
MS		
1,578	didn't really answer	
SS		
MS		

1,579	knew in advance	
SS		
MS		
1,580	had prior knowledge of	
SS		
MS		
1,581	know full well that	
SS		
MS		
1,582	as a courtesy to	
SS		
MS		
1,583	as a favour to	
SS		
MS		
1,584	in any way shape or form	
SS		
MS		

1,585	feel compelled to	
SS		
MS		
1,586	it almost sounds like	
SS		
MS		
1,587	never ever happened	
SS		
MS		
1,588	after the results	
SS		
MS		
1,589	unashamed of	
SS		
MS		
1,590	steer clear of	
SS		
MS		

1,591	left in awe	
SS		
MS		
1,592	interrupted by	
SS		
MS		
1,593	fall for	
SS		
MS		
1,594	not responsible for	
SS		
MS		
1,595	have a say in	
SS		
MS		
1,596	rethink how	
SS		
MS		

1,597	seek ways to	
SS		
MS		
1,598	do a good job of	
SS		
MS		
1,599	become a habit	
SS		
MS		
1,600	start exercising	
SS		
MS		
1,601	quit smoking	
SS		
MS		
1,602	care about the future	
SS		
MS		

1,603	would rather have	
SS		
MS		
1,604	value immediate rewards	
SS		
MS		
1,605	not altogether irrational	
SS		
MS		
1,606	would rather have	
SS		
MS		
1,607	see the numbers go up	
SS		
MS		
1,608	announced the release of	
SS		
MS		

1,609	come clean about	
SS		
MS		
1,610	even though there were	
SS		
MS		
1,611	to the utmost	
SS		
MS		
1,612	rattle X with	
SS		
MS		
1,613	capture the difficulty of	
SS		
MS		
1,614	rarely brag about	
SS		
MS		

1,615	already facing	
SS		
MS		
1,616	so anguished	
SS		
MS		
1,617	is a danger to	
SS		
MS		
1,618	put it most bluntly	
SS		
MS		
1,619	one of the staunchest supporters of	
SS		
MS		
1,620	offer a helping hand	
SS		
MS		

1,621	at every step along the way	
SS		
MS		
1,622	never would have thought	
SS		
MS		
1,623	get rid of	
SS		
MS		
1,624	don't want anyone to know	
SS		
MS		
1,625	continue the discussion	
SS		
MS		
1,626	done a lot of damage	
SS		
MS		

1,627	watch out for	
SS		
MS		
1,628	just don't know yet	
SS		
MS		
1,629	speak out against	
SS		
MS		
1,630	place blame on	
SS		
MS		
1,631	a range of	
SS		
MS		
1,632	optimistic about	
SS		
MS		

1,633	critical of	
SS		
MS		
1,634	hammer out a deal	
SS		
MS		
1,635	about to do	
SS		
MS		
1,636	sever ties	
SS		
MS		
1,637	postpone finalizing	
SS		
MS		
1,638	do damage	
SS		
MS		

1,639	tamp down expectations	
SS		
MS		
1,640	unlikely to see	
SS		
MS		
1,641	ought to be	
SS		
MS		
1,642	business activities	
SS		
MS		
1,643	not a household name	
SS		
MS		
1,644	for good reason	
SS		
MS		

1,645	sounds unfamiliar	
SS		
MS		
1,646	deserve to have	
SS		
MS		
1,647	start hearing rumors about	
SS		
MS		
1,648	never informed	
SS		
MS		
1,649	it is highly impossible	
SS		
MS		
1,650	break with the habit of	
SS		
MS		

1,651	proven untrue	
SS		
MS		
1,652	suffer huge repercussions	
SS		
MS		
1,653	step away from	
SS		
MS		
1,654	the real reason	
SS		
MS		
1,655	beyond belief	
SS		
MS		
1,656	become numb	
SS		
MS		

1,657	find the courage to	
SS		
MS		
1,658	vent about	
SS		
MS		
1,659	had doubts	
SS		
MS		
1,660	mutual friend	
SS		
MS		
1,661	a happy relationship	
SS		
MS		
1,662	refused to answer questions on	
SS		
MS		

1,663	did not tell	
SS		
MS		
1,664	the trouble with	
SS		
MS		
1,665	a minor transgression	
SS		
MS		
1,666	nearly impossible	
SS		
MS		
1,667	deeply frustrated with	
SS		
MS		
1,668	boiling with anger	
SS		
MS		

1,669	really needed	
SS		
MS		
1,670	too big to ignore	
SS		
MS		
1,671	sordid affair	
SS		
MS		
1,672	hard-pressed to understand	
SS		
MS		
1,653	worst nightmare	
SS		
MS		
1,674	adhere to	
SS		
MS		

1,675	claim that	
SS		
MS		
1,676	how unusual is it to	
SS		
MS		
1,677	grip on reality	
SS		
MS		
1,678	intricate questions	
SS		
MS		
1,679	embrace of	
SS		
MS		
1,680	wrap up	
SS		
MS		

1,681	had a lot of information	
SS		
MS		
1,682	bolstered by	
SS		
MS		
1,683	understand more now	
SS		
MS		
1,684	late at night	
SS		
MS		
1,685	know more about	
SS		
MS		
1,686	seems out of place	
SS		
MS		

1,687	seems awkward	
SS		
MS		
1,688	has come into focus	
SS		
MS		
1,689	an accurate response	
SS		
MS		
1,690	a nothing burger	
SS		
MS		
1,691	clearly agitated about	
SS		
MS		
1,692	growing angry	
SS		
MS		

1,693	legal trouble	
SS		
MS		
1,694	stewing about	
SS		
MS		
1,695	fairly upbeat about	
SS		
MS		
1,696	apply discipline	
SS		
MS		
1,697	daily goals	
SS		
MS		
1,698	fuel disappointment	
SS		
MS		

1,699	feel passionate about	
SS		
MS		
1,700	very frightening	
SS		
MS		
1,701	a top target of	
SS		
MS		
1,702	the eagerness to	
SS		
MS		
1,703	a strong case could be made for	
SS		
MS		
1,704	treading close to	
SS		
MS		

1,705	it won't take all that much	
SS		
MS		
1,706	deep down inside	
SS		
MS		
1,707	feel limitless	
SS		
MS		
1,708	not take (something) seriously	
SS		
MS		
1,709	not a shortcut to	
SS		
MS		
1,710	deeply understand	
SS		
MS		

1,711	a full schedule	
SS		
MS		
1,712	use the same technique	
SS		
MS		
1,713	stand on a knife edge	
SS		
MS		
1,714	the first requisite	
SS		
MS		
1,715	in good repute	
SS		
MS		
1,716	takes time to	
SS		
MS		

1,717	doesn't have the support of	
SS		
MS		
1,718	get rid of	
SS		
MS		
1,719	does appear to	
SS		
MS		
1,720	is/was cavalier with	
SS		
MS		
1,721	report directly to	
SS		
MS		
1,722	warning signals	
SS		
MS		

1,723	the correct version of	
SS		
MS		
1,724	undivided attention	
SS		
MS		
1,725	a hopeful statement	
SS		
MS		
1,726	react to	
SS		
MS		
1,727	stuck around	
SS		
MS		
1,728	going places	
SS		
MS		

1,729	own stock in	
SS		
MS		
1,730	never happened to	
SS		
MS		
1,731	present at the meeting	
SS		
MS		
1,732	misleading statement	
SS		
MS		
1,733	it is problematic	
SS		
MS		
1,734	a pathological liar	
SS		
MS		

1,735	the focus of X is on	
SS		
MS		
1,736	a proven liar	
SS		
MS		
1,737	in great detail	
SS		
MS		
1,738	bad news for	
SS		
MS		
1,739	go off the rails	
SS		
MS		
1,740	directly impacted by	
SS		
MS		

1,741	meet one on one	
SS		
MS		
1,742	do one's level best	
SS		
MS		
1,743	rather contentious	
SS		
MS		
1,744	not in line with	
SS		
MS		
1,745	a difficult problem	
SS		
MS		
1,746	need to be better	
SS		
MS		

1,747	very difficult to	
SS		
MS		
1,748	unintended consequence	
SS		
MS		
1,749	mindful of	
SS		
MS		
1,750	backtrack on	
SS		
MS		
1,751	key issue	
SS		
MS		
1,752	walk away from	
SS		
MS		

1,753	do someone's bidding	
SS		
MS		
1,754	the kinds of	
SS		
MS		
1,755	just an effort to	
SS		
MS		
1,756	a pretext to	
SS		
MS		
1,757	not complied with	
SS		
MS		
1,758	try to intimidate (someone)	
SS		
MS		

1,759	ought to be ready	
SS		
MS		
1,760	right on target	
SS		
MS		
1,761	stand with (someone)	
SS		
MS		
1,762	a battery of questions	
SS		
MS		
1,763	an odd way of	
SS		
MS		
1,764	refuse to leave	
SS		
MS		

1,765	ask questions of (someone)	
SS		
MS		
1,766	at some point	
SS		
MS		
1,767	a little uncomfortable	
SS		
MS		
1,768	denied knowing anything about	
SS		
MS		
1,769	dredge up	
SS		
MS		
1,770	totally irrelevant	
SS		
MS		

1,771	on a daily basis	
SS		
MS		
1,772	doesn't prove	
SS		
MS		
1,773	telling the truth	
SS		
MS		
1,774	not healthy	
SS		
MS		
1,775	could have done	
SS		
MS		
1,776	bragged about	
SS		
MS		

1,777	what limits	
SS		
MS		
1,778	fail in school	
SS		
MS		
1,779	easy to use	
SS		
MS		
1,780	important for	
SS		
MS		
1,781	lead to	
SS		
MS		
1,782	gainful employment	
SS		
MS		

1,783	worked hard	
SS		
MS		
1,784	a harsh reality	
SS		
MS		
1,785	run out of	
SS		
MS		
1,786	betrayal of	
SS		
MS		
1,787	certainly start with	
SS		
MS		
1,788	overcome with	
SS		
MS		

1,789	bail out	
SS		
MS		
1,790	angry about	
SS		
MS		
1,791	very interested to see	
SS		
MS		
1,792	in advance of	
SS		
MS		
1,793	overriding impression	
SS		
MS		
1,794	immediate response	
SS		
MS		

1,795	failed to keep (one's) promise	
SS		
MS		
1,796	push back against	
SS		
MS		
1,797	deep concern for	
SS		
MS		
1,798	intertwine with	
SS		
MS		
1,799	extremely sympathetic to	
SS		
MS		
1,800	to prison	
SS		
MS		

1,801	in jail	
SS		
MS		
1,802	always believed	
SS		
MS		
1,803	fully in charge of	
SS		
MS		
1,804	one and the same	
SS		
MS		
1,805	creating doubt	
SS		
MS		
1,806	not unlike	
SS		
MS		

1,807	at the same time	
SS		
MS		
1,808	have tremendous faith in	
SS		
MS		
1,809	doesn't tell the truth about	
SS		
MS		
1,810	there's not a lot of	
SS		
MS		
1,811	talk turkey	
SS		
MS		
1,812	too uncomfortable	
SS		
MS		

1,813	fire back	
SS		
MS		
1,814	announce a break from	
SS		
MS		
1,815	get hit with	
SS		
MS		
1,816	too uncontrollable	
SS		
MS		
1,817	can't speak for	
SS		
MS		
1,818	so embarrassing	
SS		
MS		

1,819	eat properly	
SS		
MS		
1,820	so brazen	
SS		
MS		
1,821	decided that	
SS		
MS		
1,822	have the best intentions	
SS		
MS		
1,823	it's clear that	
SS		
MS		
1,824	still believe	
SS		
MS		

1,825	on one's toes	
SS		
MS		
1,826	defer to	
SS		
MS		
1,827	quick to retaliate	
SS		
MS		
1,828	put everything on pause	
SS		
MS		
1,829	measured in (one's) response	
SS		
MS		
1,830	says nothing at all about	
SS		
MS		

1,831	assert that	
SS		
MS		
1,832	feel victimized	
SS		
MS		
1,833	sounds reasonable	
SS		
MS		
1,834	no one to blame but	
SS		
MS		
1,835	out of business	
SS		
MS		
1,836	in business	
SS		
MS		

1,837	blatant disregard for	
SS		
MS		
1,838	growing concern about	
SS		
MS		
1,839	a serious investigation	
SS		
MS		
1,840	on a daily basis	
SS		
MS		
1,841	productive discussion	
SS		
MS		
1,842	link back to	
SS		
MS		

1,843	sceptical of	
SS		
MS		
1,844	just awful	
SS		
MS		
1,845	a reference to	
SS		
MS		
1,846	mosaic of evidence	
SS		
MS		
1,847	currently involved with	
SS		
MS		
1,848	take exception with	
SS		
MS		

1,849	move past (something)	
SS		
MS		
1,850	have a debate	
SS		
MS		
1,851	tension between A and B	
SS		
MS		
1,852	on shaky ground	
SS		
MS		
1,853	stick with	
SS		
MS		
1,854	cast aspersions on	
SS		
MS		

1,855	get back to	
SS		
MS		
1,856	garner sympathy	
SS		
MS		
1,857	mixed reaction	
SS		
MS		
1,858	have a fairly good understanding of	
SS		
MS		
1,859	focus sharply	
SS		
MS		
1,860	a horrific comment	
SS		
MS		

1,861	basic issues	
SS		
MS		
1,862	an assault on	
SS		
MS		
1,863	a side show	
SS		
MS		
1,864	material misrepresentation	
SS		
MS		
1,865	interfere in	
SS		
MS		
1,866	never took the time	
SS		
MS		

1,867	a foregone conclusion	
SS		
MS		
1,868	have a great idea	
SS		
MS		
1,869	have a few thoughts on	
SS		
MS		
1,870	at odds over	
SS		
MS		
1,871	not a good idea	
SS		
MS		
1,872	preside over	
SS		
MS		

1,873	misunderstanding of	
SS		
MS		
1,874	a lot more tasteful	
SS		
MS		
1,875	simply unnecessary	
SS		
MS		
1,876	one of the greatest	
SS		
MS		
1,877	close the gap	
SS		
MS		
1,878	draw together	
SS		
MS		

1,879	argue strenuously	
SS		
MS		
1,880	show support for	
SS		
MS		
1,881	strongly against	
SS		
MS		
1,882	provide fodder for	
SS		
MS		
1,883	throw cold water on	
SS		
MS		
1,884	has difficulty with	
SS		
MS		

1,885	sit down with	
SS		
MS		
1,886	need to be	
SS		
MS		
1,887	a little suspicious	
SS		
MS		
1,888	taken aback by	
SS		
MS		
1,889	much preferable to	
SS		
MS		
1,890	much prefer	
SS		
MS		

1,891	remain firmly behind	
SS		
MS		
1,892	believable answer	
SS		
MS		
1,893	feeling the heat	
SS		
MS		
1,894	take charge	
SS		
MS		
1,895	reluctant to	
SS		
MS		
1,896	trample on	
SS		
MS		

1,897	big on (something)	
SS		
MS		
1,898	more lengthy	
SS		
MS		
1,899	even before	
SS		
MS		
1,900	is/was afoot	
SS		
MS		
1,901	travel alone to	
SS		
MS		
1,902	those who believe in	
SS		
MS		

1,903	the greatest threat to	
SS		
MS		
1,904	barely talk to	
SS		
MS		
1,905	substantial evidence	
SS		
MS		
1,906	has long been regarded as	
SS		
MS		
1,907	out of spite	
SS		
MS		
1,908	upset at	
SS		
MS		

1,909	call the shots	
SS		
MS		
1,910	doesn't pass the smell test	
SS		
MS		
1,911	taken aback	
SS		
MS		
1,912	multiple sources	
SS		
MS		
1,913	work hand in glove	
SS		
MS		
1,914	changed completely	
SS		
MS		

1,915	out of bounds	
SS		
MS		
1,916	a constant refrain	
SS		
MS		
1,917	make a request of	
SS		
MS		
1,918	the knives are out	
SS		
MS		
1,919	spouting off	
SS		
MS		
1,920	normal use of	
SS		
MS		

1,921	get (one's) story straight	
SS		
MS		
1,922	done nothing to minimize	
SS		
MS		
1,923	out of trouble	
SS		
MS		
1,924	make no sense	
SS		
MS		
1,925	white-collar crime	
SS		
MS		
1,926	express doubt	
SS		
MS		

1,927	run afoul of	
SS		
MS		
1,928	deep six (something)	
SS		
MS		
1,929	so disrespectful to	
SS		
MS		
1,930	downright chilling	
SS		
MS		
1,931	look at (someone/something) with a jaundiced eye	
SS		
MS		
1,932	free of	
SS		
MS		

1,933	evolve over time	
SS		
MS		
1,934	have no choice but to	
SS		
MS		
1,935	in my life	
SS		
MS		
1,936	work directly with	
SS		
MS		
1,937	be a part of	
SS		
MS		
1,938	a frantic search for	
SS		
MS		

1,939	ongoing litigation	
SS		
MS		
1,940	preventable harm	
SS		
MS		
1,941	switch tactics	
SS		
MS		
1,942	a tipping point	
SS		
MS		
1,943	social awareness	
SS		
MS		
1,944	lose a step	
SS		
MS		

1,945	deeply care for	
SS		
MS		
1,946	stunning disaster	
SS		
MS		
1,947	a desperate search for	
SS		
MS		
1,948	there is very little	
SS		
MS		
1,949	too much to bear	
SS		
MS		
1,950	keep a close eye on	
SS		
MS		

1,951	I would say	
SS		
MS		
1,952	incredibly funny	
SS		
MS		
1,953	never quite seen	
SS		
MS		
1,954	incredibly gifted	
SS		
MS		
1,955	make life easier	
SS		
MS		
1,956	stuck in traffic	
SS		
MS		

1,957	display any sign of	
SS		
MS		
1,958	genuinely believe	
SS		
MS		
1,959	would not end well	
SS		
MS		
1,960	really irresponsible	
SS		
MS		
1,961	over the past X weeks	
SS		
MS		
1,962	muddy the waters	
SS		
MS		

1,963	deeply uncomfortable	
SS		
MS		
1,964	right after	
SS		
MS		
1,965	lost in the shuffle	
SS		
MS		
1,966	no daylight between A and B	
SS		
MS		
1,967	watch agog	
SS		
MS		
1,968	a permanent record	
SS		
S		

1,969	a terrifying time	
SS		
MS		
1,970	tough question	
SS		
MS		
1,971	publicly release	
SS		
MS		
1,972	a high degree of expertise	
SS		
MS		
1,973	come forward	
SS		
MS		
1,974	the source of	
SS		
MS		

1,975	ongoing litigation	
SS		
MS		
1,976	in a vise	
SS		
MS		
1,977	it's neither here nor there	
SS		
MS		
1,978	unmet needs	
SS		
MS		
1,979	grapple with	
SS		
MS		
1,980	bald-faced lie	
SS		
MS		

1,981	illegal contribution	
SS		
MS		
1,982	no wiggle room	
SS		
MS		
1,983	conflicting statements	
SS		
MS		
1,984	feel aggrieved	
SS		
MS		
1,985	pull the curtain back	
SS		
MS		
1,986	come to grips with	
SS		
MS		

1,987	first met	
SS		
MS		
1,988	less guarded	
SS		
MS		
1,989	a price to pay	
SS		
MS		
1,990	did not take a hit for	
SS		
MS		
1,991	build up to	
SS		
MS		
1,992	more frenetic	
SS		
MS		

1,993	out of the loop	
SS		
MS		
1,994	blurring of the lines	
SS		
MS		
1,995	something as significant as	
SS		
MS		
1,996	dysfunctional household	
SS		
MS		
1,997	demolish someone's credibility	
SS		
MS		
1,998	press (someone) on (something)	
SS		
MS		

1,999	get away with	
SS		
MS		
2,000	since deleted	
SS		
MS		
2,001	unlike any other	
SS		
MS		
2,002	at a given moment	
SS		
MS		
2,003	in the aftermath of	
SS		
MS		
2,004	the very best information	
SS		
MS		

2,005	better anticipate	
SS		
MS		
2,006	unwelcome reception	
SS		
MS		
2,007	nothing to boast about	
SS		
MS		
2,008	could not help but notice	
SS		
MS		
2,009	take someone at her word	
SS		
MS		
2,010	vast numbers of people	
SS		
MS		

2,011	a serious point	
SS		
MS		
2,012	by persuasion	
SS		
MS		
2,013	make no apology	
SS		
MS		
2,014	adopted by	
SS		
MS		
2,015	the determination to	
SS		
MS		
2,016	in shock	
SS		
MS		

2,017	brushed off (one's) skills	
SS		
MS		
2,018	received a phone call	
SS		
MS		
2,019	finally prove	
SS		
MS		
2,020	back out	
SS		
MS		
2,021	keep one's pulse on	
SS		
MS		
2,022	the core problem is	
SS		
MS		

2,023	could be true	
SS		
MS		
2,024	so high that	
SS		
MS		
2,025	did surprisingly well	
SS		
MS		
2,026	not truthful about	
SS		
MS		
2,027	over the last generation	
SS		
MS		
2,028	nightmare scenario	
SS		
MS		

2,029	open up	
SS		
MS		
2,030	interest in	
SS		
MS		
2,031	in the coming week	
SS		
MS		
2,032	an exemplar of	
SS		
MS		
2,033	a sense of community	
SS		
MS		
2,034	a whole host of	
SS		
MS		

2,035	stepping down	
SS		
MS		
2,036	under suspicion of	
SS		
MS		
2,037	is/was on display	
SS		
MS		
2,038	armed with	
SS		
MS		
2,039	a not uncommon practice	
SS		
MS		
2,040	in addition to	
SS		
MS		

2,041	it is very important that	
SS		
MS		
2,042	call the police	
SS		
MS		
2,043	uncharted territory	
SS		
MS		
2,044	give license to	
SS		
MS		
2,045	beg to differ	
SS		
MS		
2,046	come to expect	
SS		
MS		

2,047	take center stage	
SS		
MS		
2,048	out of control	
SS		
MS		
2,049	get caught up in	
SS		
MS		
2,050	innocent people	
SS		
MS		
2,051	begin with	
SS		
MS		
2,052	go beyond	
SS		
MS		

2,053	cast out	
SS		
MS		
2,054	face pressure	
SS		
MS		
2,055	hugely popular	
SS		
MS		
2,056	near-constant presence	
SS		
MS		
2,057	not too impressed by	
SS		
MS		
2,058	not affected by	
SS		
MS		

2,059	soften the ground for	
SS		
MS		
2,060	not much of a sense of	
SS		
MS		
2,061	the only (thing) that matters	
SS		
MS		
2,062	horrified that	
SS		
MS		
2,063	the rightful owner	
SS		
MS		
2,064	make arguments	
SS		
MS		

2,065	real effect	
SS		
MS		
2,066	part of the same story	
SS		
MS		
2,067	there clearly still is	
SS		
MS		
2,068	material compensation	
SS		
MS		
2,069	correlates very strongly with	
SS		
MS		
2,070	a complicated question	
SS		
MS		

2,071	appropriate for	
SS		
MS		
2,072	call into question	
SS		
MS		
2,073	meant to	
SS		
MS		
2,074	start working on	
SS		
MS		
2,075	aware of	
SS		
MS		
2,076	enraged by	
SS		
MS		

2,077	split apart by	
SS		
MS		
2,078	open to interpretation	
SS		
MS		
2,079	bend over backwards for	
SS		
MS		
2,080	point out	
SS		
MS		
2,081	a decent job	
SS		
MS		
2,082	passionate commitment	
SS		
MS		

2,083	without regard to	
SS		
MS		
2,084	not unfamiliar with	
SS		
MS		
2,085	equivocal response	
SS		
MS		
2,086	hard to overestimate	
SS		
MS		
2,087	stand up to	
SS		
MS		
2,088	one of the hallmarks of	
SS		
MS		

2,089	a brilliant coup	
SS		
MS		
2,090	less important than	
SS		
MS		
2,091	not without risk	
SS		
MS		
2,092	no desire to	
SS		
MS		
2,093	derive from	
SS		
MS		
2,094	does not work any more	
SS		
MS		

2,095	a fixed idea	
SS		
MS		
2,096	predictable results	
SS		
MS		
2,097	out of favor	
SS		
MS		
2,098	favoured treatment	
SS		
MS		
2,099	increasingly neglected	
SS		
MS		
2,100	to the chagrin of	
SS		
MS		

2,101	drained of	
SS		
MS		
2,102	hold dear	
SS		
MS		
2,103	reward for	
SS		
MS		
2,104	has much to do with	
SS		
MS		
2,105	the necessity for	
SS		
MS		
2,106	accepted as a given	
SS		
MS		

2,107	instrumental in	
SS		
MS		
2,108	feel sympathy for	
SS		
MS		
2,109	gain momentum	
SS		
MS		
2,110	try to prove	
SS		
MS		
2,111	overtaken by	
SS		
MS		
2,112	there is a possibility for	
SS		
MS		

2,113	perfectly happy to	
SS		
MS		
2,114	wage war against	
SS		
MS		
2,115	closely identified with	
SS		
MS		
2.116	close ranks around	
SS		
MS		
2,117	do a deep dive	
SS		
MS		
2,118	place stress on	
SS		
MS		

2,119	a worrisome indifference	
SS		
MS		
2,120	not long after	
SS		
MS		
2,121	abrupt about face	
SS		
MS		
2,122	caught up with	
SS		
MS		
2,123	become distressed	
SS		
MS		
2,124	carefully chosen	
SS		
MS		

2,125	saddle someone with	
SS		
MS		
2,126	it is generally agreed that	
SS		
MS		
2,127	try to conceal (something)	
SS		
MS		
2,128	a fresh injustice to	
SS		
MS		
2,129	collective responsibility	
SS		
MS		
2,130	feel very strongly about	
SS		
MS		

2,131	seriously confront the idea	
SS		
MS		
2,132	contacted by	
SS		
MS		
2,133	particularly problematic	
SS		
MS		
2,134	put up a strong fight	
SS		
MS		
2,135	getting worse and worse	
SS		
MS		
2,136	at the behest of	
SS		
MS		

2,137	genuine dialogue	
SS		
MS		
2,138	it is difficult partly because	
SS		
MS		
2,139	a clear path to	
SS		
MS		
2,140	come off like	
SS		
MS		
2,141	does not look well	
SS		
MS		
2,142	utter contempt for	
SS		
MS		

2,143	enormously destructive	
SS		
MS		
2,144	winding down	
SS		
MS		
2,145	in defense of	
SS		
MS		
2,146	concerned about	
SS		
MS		
2,147	in an awkward spot	
SS		
MS		
2,148	in lieu of	
SS		
MS		

2,149	reaction from	
SS		
MS		
2,150	remain safe	
SS		
MS		
2,151	let the cat out of the bag	
SS		
MS		
2,152	in the offing	
SS		
MS		
2,153	nobody knew	
SS		
MS		
2,154	look up to	
SS		
MS		

2,155	every other day	
SS		
MS		
2,156	on the streets	
SS		
MS		
2,157	fend off	
SS		
MS		
2,158	a worthy event	
SS		
MS		
2,159	admit to	
SS		
MS		
2,160	humbly learning	
SS		
MS		

2,161	in cahoots with	
SS		
MS		
2,162	the most shameful	
SS		
MS		
2,163	continuing tradition	
SS		
MS		
2,164	have a dispute with	
SS		
MS		
2,165	it's well worth emphasizing that	
SS		
MS		
2,166	terms of the agreement	
SS		
MS		

2,167	not interested in	
SS		
MS		
2,168	standard bearer	
SS		
MS		
2,169	utter nonsense	
SS		
MS		
2,170	a moment of shame	
SS		
MS		
2,171	the primary role	
SS		
MS		
2,172	reinforce a point	
SS		
MS		

2,173	did damage to	
SS		
MS		
2,174	social mobility	
SS		
MS		
2,175	personal responsibility	
SS		
MS		
2,176	a good impulse	
SS		
MS		
2,177	partial truth	
SS		
MS		
2,178	as equal partners	
SS		
MS		

2,179	fully loaded for bear	
SS		
MS		
2,180	in a curious way	
SS		
MS		
2,181	an elegant way of	
SS		
MS		
2,182	for the benefit of	
SS		
MS		
2,183	the authenticity of	
SS		
MS		
2,184	in furtherance of	
SS		
MS		

2,185	all indications are that	
SS		
MS		
2,186	impeccable credentials	
SS		
MS		
2,187	a blot on	
SS		
MS		
2,188	fall short of	
SS		
MS		
2,189	bear in mind	
SS		
MS		
2,190	abandon any hope of	
SS		
MS		

2,191	tacit acknowledgment of	
SS		
MS		
2,192	riddled with	
SS		
MS		
2,193	mind-numbing work	
SS		
MS		
2,194	break the chain of	
SS		
MS		
2,195	flagrantly violate	
SS		
MS		
2,196	so long as	
SS		
MS		

2,197	revert to	
SS		
MS		
2,198	egregious abuse	
SS		
MS		
2,199	absolutely heartwarming	
SS		
MS		
2,200	disturbing tremors	
SS		
MS		
2,201	do not disdain	
SS		
MS		
2,202	the very fact that	
SS		
MS		

2,203	impossibly narrow set of options	
SS		
MS		
2,204	absolutely fascinating	
SS		
MS		
2,205	prohibition against	
SS		
MS		
2,206	compulsory teaching of	
SS		
MS		
2,207	the best possible chance	
SS		
MS		
2,208	a badge of civilization	
SS		
MS		

2,209	pose a threat to	
SS		
MS		
2,210	need to step back	
SS		
MS		
2,211	do everything humanely possible	
SS		
MS		
2,212	throw someone under the bus	
SS		
MS		
2,213	fill a void	
SS		
MS		
2,214	proper skills	
SS		
MS		

2,215	an astonishing answer	
SS		
MS		
2,216	much less about	
SS		
MS		
2,217	incredibly unpleasant	
SS		
MS		
2,218	important to realize	
SS		
MS		
2,219	pose a risk	
SS		
MS		
2,220	central to	
SS		
MS		

2,221	warning signs	
SS		
MS		
2,222	over the course of	
SS		
MS		
2,223	all of a sudden	
SS		
MS		
2,224	immensely important	
SS		
MS		
2,225	warm up to	
SS		
MS		
2,226	poison the well	
SS		
MS		

2,227	a rather crude way of	
SS		
MS		
2,228	the underbelly of	
SS		
MS		
2,229	led to believe	
SS		
MS		
2,230	unfamiliar with	
SS		
MS		
2,231	totally disagree with	
SS		
MS		
2,232	take strong issue with	
SS		
MS		

2,233	stubborn problem	
SS		
MS		
2,234	different ways of	
SS		
MS		
2,235	in many respects	
SS		
MS		
2,236	single out	
SS		
MS		
2,237	a widespread supposition	
SS		
MS		
2,238	wish to be	
SS		
MS		

2,239	seem to be very reluctant	
SS		
MS		
2,240	a respite from	
SS		
MS		
2,241	deny foreknowledge of	
SS		
MS		
2,242	bear a resemblance to	
SS		
MS		
2,243	terribly betrayed	
SS		
MS		
2,244	have foreknowledge of	
SS		
MS		

2,245	win by a landslide	
SS		
MS		
2,246	an exact echo of	
SS		
MS		
2,247	pretty ridiculous	
SS		
MS		
2,248	see no evidence	
SS		
MS		
2,249	held out hope	
SS		
MS		
2,250	in a matter of years	
SS		
MS		

2,251	always up for	
SS		
MS		
2,252	far less stringent than	
SS		
MS		
2,253	manoeuvre (something)	
SS		
MS		
2,254	frown on	
SS		
MS		
2,255	subservience to	
SS		
MS		
2,256	have to ask	
SS		
MS		

2,257	no longer	
SS		
MS		
2,258	so preposterous	
SS		
MS		
2,259	it may very well be that	
SS		
MS		
2,260	reverse course	
SS		
MS		
2,261	a tense moment	
SS		
MS		
2,262	tough talk	
SS		
MS		

2,263	talk plenty about	
SS		
MS		
2,264	there's no real threat	
SS		
MS		
2,265	poised to	
SS		
MS		
2,266	raise the risk of	
SS		
MS		
2,267	it's worth noting that	
SS		
MS		
2,268	there comes a time when	
SS		
MS		

2,269	put pressure on	
SS		
MS		
2,270	embark on	
SS		
MS		
2,271	likened to	
SS		
MS		
2,272	does not meet reality	
SS		
MS		
2,273	very tough on	
SS		
MS		
2,274	made it impossible for	
SS		
MS		

2,275	embarrassed by	
SS		
MS		
2,276	would be foolish to	
SS		
MS		
2,277	cause a revolt against	
SS		
MS		
2,278	change the subject	
SS		
MS		
2,279	in attendance	
SS		
MS		
2,280	deserve more scrutiny	
SS		
MS		

2,281	some tough issues	
SS		
MS		
2,282	better at	
SS		
MS		
2,283	extremely talented	
SS		
MS		
2,284	zeal for	
SS		
MS		
2,285	not unique to	
SS		
MS		
2,286	have a do-over	
SS		
MS		

2,287	diminished role	
SS		
MS		
2,288	admiration for	
SS		
MS		
2,289	with empathy	
SS		
MS		
2,290	spar with	
SS		
MS		
2,291	under pressure from	
SS		
MS		
2,292	probably didn't think	
SS		
MS		

2,293	question X about	
SS		
MS		
2,294	never implemented	
SS		
MS		
2,295	filled with	
SS		
MS		
2,296	if provoked	
SS		
MS		
2,297	a continuation of	
SS		
MS		
2,298	a huge blow to	
SS		
MS		

2,299	very firm on	
SS		
MS		
2,300	expressed opposition to	
SS		
MS		
2,301	connect to	
SS		
MS		
2,302	a magical moment	
SS		
MS		
2,303	not involved	
SS		
MS		
2,304	handle conflict	
SS		
MS		

2,305	board a plane	
SS		
MS		
2,306	barely blinked	
SS		
MS		
2,307	sample some X	
SS		
MS		
2,308	cry out for	
SS		
MS		
2,309	suffer consequences	
SS		
MS		
2,310	tensions between A and B	
SS		
MS		

2,311	going to go from	
SS		
MS		
2,312	the first time that	
SS		
MS		
2,313	dramatically curtail	
SS		
MS		
2,314	in a similar situation	
SS		
MS		
2,315	make enough to	
SS		
MS		
2,316	have a steady job	
SS		
MS		

2,317	stuck with	
SS		
MS		
2,318	from a distance	
SS		
MS		
2,319	in the hope of	
SS		
MS		
2,320	it's true enough	
SS		
MS		
2,321	without remembering	
SS		
MS		
2,322	may explain why	
SS		
MS		

2,323	has had a significant impact on	
SS		
MS		
2,324	emerge from	
SS		
MS		
2,325	skimp on	
SS		
MS		
2,326	aim to	
SS		
MS		
2,327	a certain amount of	
SS		
MS		
2,328	so reliant on	
SS		
MS		

2,329	need at least	
SS		
MS		
2,330	decline of	
SS		
MS		
2,331	could suffer	
SS		
MS		
2,332	have larger implications	
SS		
MS		
2,333	don't contribute	
SS		
MS		
2,334	the current wave of	
SS		
MS		

2,335	what could befall	
SS		
MS		
2,336	a more accurate measure	
SS		
MS		
2,337	not much of an appetite for	
SS		
MS		
2,338	without the ability to	
SS		
MS		
2,339	take time off	
SS		
MS		
2,340	can be particularly hard on	
SS		
MS		

2,341	can't quit	
SS		
MS		
2,342	couldn't afford	
SS		
MS		
2,343	relied on	
SS		
MS		
2,344	impose on	
SS		
MS		
2,345	the answer to	
SS		
MS		
2,346	give (one) pause	
SS		
MS		

2,347	issued a statement	
SS		
MS		
2,348	amazed that	
SS		
MS		
2,349	on the verge of	
SS		
MS		
2,350	on the agenda	
SS		
MS		
2,351	in every way	
SS		
MS		
2,352	feel threatened by	
SS		
MS		

2,353	keep food on the table	
SS		
MS		
2,354	feel a little more	
SS		
MS		
2,355	reduce the amount of	
SS		
MS		
2,356	much more stable	
SS		
MS		
2,357	more help	
SS		
MS		
2,358	trust to	
SS		
MS		

2,359	it's hardly as if	
SS		
MS		
2,360	curtailed by	
SS		
MS		
2,361	more important than	
SS		
MS		
2,362	some people can	
SS		
MS		
2,363	for many people	
SS		
MS		
2,364	recently finished	
SS		
MS		

2,365	leaning in	
SS		
MS		
2,366	it is fair to say	
SS		
MS		
2,367	would have had to	
SS		
MS		
2,368	lose the edge	
SS		
MS		
2,369	by any stretch of the imagination	
SS		
MS		
2,370	so ridiculous that	
SS		
MS		

2,371	doesn't seem like	
SS		
MS		
2,372	many facets	
SS		
MS		
2,373	at any given moment	
SS		
MS		
2,374	offer immediate access to	
SS		
MS		
2,375	unless you put effort into	
SS		
MS		
2,376	all in one stretch	
SS		
MS		

2,377	get reinforced	
SS		
MS		
2,378	get irritated	
SS		
MS		
2,379	stand no chance of	
SS		
MS		
2,380	acquire information	
SS		
MS		
2,381	credited with	
SS		
MS		
2,382	accessible to	
SS		
MS		

2,383	go far beyond	
SS		
MS		
2,384	human understanding	
SS		
MS		
2,385	run the risk of	
SS		
MS		
2,386	shaped by	
SS		
MS		
2,387	overwhelmed by	
SS		
MS		
2,388	diverted from	
SS		
MS		

2,389	threaten to	
SS		
MS		
2,390	relevant to	
SS		
MS		
2,391	reckon with	
SS		
MS		
2,392	powered by	
SS		
MS		
2,393	marks a stunning reversal for	
SS		
MS		
2,394	disappointed by	
SS		
MS		

2,395	in upheaval	
SS		
MS		
2,396	delighted by	
SS		
MS		
2,397	within a measurable period	
SS		
MS		
2,398	seek to bring about	
SS		
MS		
2,399	confined to	
SS		
MS		
2,400	anticipate that	
SS		
MS		

2,401	disrupted by	
SS		
MS		
2,402	about to retire	
SS		
MS		
2,403	take over	
SS		
MS		
2,404	feeling guilty	
SS		
MS		
2,405	lay it on the line	
SS		
MS		
2,406	pretty shocking	
SS		
MS		

2,407	scientific evidence	
SS		
MS		
2,408	a rare place	
SS		
MS		
2,409	get a lot worse	
SS		
MS		
2,410	no running water	
SS		
MS		
2,411	get so little publicity	
SS		
MS		
2,412	in a terrible mood	
SS		
MS		

2,413	made in sincerity	
SS		
MS		
2,414	how naive	
SS		
MS		
2,415	begin to address	
SS		
MS		
2,416	first and foremost	
SS		
MS		
2,417	meet with	
SS		
MS		
2,418	is/was obviously ridiculous	
SS		
MS		

2,419	criticism of	
SS		
MS		
2,420	in exchange for	
SS		
MS		
2,421	fallout from	
SS		
MS		
2,422	could never survive	
SS		
MS		
2,423	as to whether	
SS		
MS		
2,424	know to be true	
SS		
MS		

2,425	made an observation	
SS		
MS		
2,426	must demand	
SS		
MS		
2,427	work closely with	
SS		
MS		
2,428	will not accept	
SS		
MS		
2,429	could happen in the future	
SS		
MS		
2,430	dismayed that	
SS		
MS		

2,431	retaliate against	
SS		
MS		
2,432	lack of information	
SS		
MS		
2,433	lasting damage	
SS		
MS		
2,434	in real time	
SS		
MS		
2,435	pay close attention to	
SS		
MS		
2,436	go rogue	
SS		
MS		

2,437	laugh at	
SS		
MS		
2,438	in an uproar	
SS		
MS		
2,439	encroach on	
SS		
MS		
2,440	collateral damage	
SS		
MS		
2,441	not a factor in	
SS		
MS		
2,442	become the norm	
SS		
MS		

2,443	came about because	
SS		
MS		
2,444	at the expense of	
SS		
MS		
2,445	attack on	
SS		
MS		
2,446	hostile to	
SS		
MS		
2,447	sampling local delicacies	
SS		
MS		
2,448	promising career	
SS		
MS		

2,449	not showing	
SS		
MS		
2,450	can't trust	
SS		
MS		
2,451	have serious questions about	
SS		
MS		
2,452	supportive of	
SS		
MS		
2,453	if you see	
SS		
MS		
2,454	satisfied with	
SS		
MS		

2,455	step into	
SS		
MS		
2,456	throw in the towel	
SS		
MS		
2,457	pick away at (one's) food	
SS		
MS		
2,458	is/was mobbed by	
SS		
MS		
2,459	thrilled about	
SS		
MS		
2,460	ill-advised move	
SS		
MS		

2,461	against all odds	
SS		
MS		
2,462	feel sick	
SS		
MS		
2,463	get an insight into	
SS		
MS		
2,464	not acceptable	
SS		
MS		
2,465	have confidence in	
SS		
MS		
2,466	over the years	
SS		
MS		

2,467	ill-gotten gains	
SS		
MS		
2,468	the intent is to	
SS		
MS		
2,469	bring attention to	
SS		
MS		
2,470	not funny	
SS		
MS		
2,471	the strongest antidote	
SS		
MS		
2,472	got worse and worse	
SS		
MS		

2,473	is/was good enough to	
SS		
MS		
2,474	make multiple attempts to	
SS		
MS		
2,475	a pathetic attempt to	
SS		
MS		
2,476	a remarkable development	
SS		
MS		
2,477	is/was independent of	
SS		
MS		
2,478	stay in touch with	
SS		
MS		

2,479	lack of understanding	
SS		
MS		
2,480	make a payment to	
SS		
MS		
2,481	is/was very troubled	
SS		
MS		
2,482	adamant about	
SS		
MS		
2,483	do right by (someone)	
SS		
MS		
2,484	get the impression that	
SS		
MS		

2,485	ongoing investigation	
SS		
MS		
2,486	cave in	
SS		
MS		
2,487	the clock is running out on	
SS		
MS		
2,488	aimed at	
SS		
MS		
2,489	does not understand	
SS		
MS		
2,490	back away from	
SS		
MS		

2,491	clear up	
SS		
MS		
2,492	deeply involved in	
SS		
MS		
2,493	don't have a clue	
SS		
MS		
2,494	it's particularly important to	
SS		
MS		
2,495	don't want to rattle the cages	
SS		
MS		
2,496	talk harshly against	
SS		
MS		

2,497	discussions are underway	
SS		
MS		
2,498	meet privately with	
SS		
MS		
2,499	go off script	
SS		
MS		
2,500	an in-depth look	
SS		
MS		
2,501	get it wrong	
SS		
MS		
2,502	very poorly	
SS		
MS		

2,503	actively participated in	
SS		
MS		
2,504	one thing is for sure	
SS		
MS		
2,505	asking questions	
SS		
MS		
2,506	a waste of time	
SS		
MS		
2,507	of interest to	
SS		
MS		
2,508	almost certainly	
SS		
MS		

2,509	question (someone's) ability	
SS		
MS		
2,510	the purpose of	
SS		
MS		
2,511	declined to comment on	
SS		
MS		
2,512	in connection with	
SS		
MS		
2,513	don't want to think too hard about	
SS		
MS		
2,514	is/was no explicable reason	
SS		
MS		

2,515	it's time for	
SS		
MS		
2,516	the clearest sign	
SS		
MS		
2,517	not surprising	
SS		
MS		
2,518	have an excuse	
SS		
MS		
2,519	lied about	
SS		
MS		
2,520	a fiery speech	
SS		
MS		

2,521	in all seriousness	
SS		
MS		
2,522	tweet about	
SS		
MS		
2,523	starting to see	
SS		
MS		
2,524	air out	
SS		
MS		
2,525	have access to	
SS		
MS		
2,526	the real challenge	
SS		
MS		

2,527	keeps getting worse	
SS		
MS		
2,528	damning evidence	
SS		
MS		
2,529	a piece of new information	
SS		
MS		
2,530	applies to	
SS		
MS		
2,531	a common thread	
SS		
MS		
2,532	not so great for	
SS		
MS		

2,533	put one's finger on	
SS		
MS		
2,534	strive after	
SS		
MS		
2,535	make a mockery of	
SS		
MS		
2,536	deliver a speech	
SS		
MS		
2,537	not fit to be	
SS		
MS		
2,538	was told that	
SS		
MS		

2,539	toe the line	
SS		
MS		
2,540	deeply disturbing	
SS		
MS		
2,541	take credit for	
SS		
MS		
2,542	learned about	
SS		
MS		
2,543	after having reflected on	
SS		
MS		
2,544	close with	
SS		
MS		

2,545	has no problem	
SS		
MS		
2,546	fall asleep	
SS		
MS		
2,547	expressed no interest	
SS		
MS		
2,548	doesn't know for certain	
SS		
MS		
2,549	get out of hand	
SS		
MS		
2,550	let slip that	
SS		
MS		

2,551	take the initiative	
SS		
MS		
2,552	untimely death	
SS		
MS		
2,553	don't know for sure	
SS		
MS		
2,554	very close friend	
SS		
MS		
2,555	finally decide	
SS		
MS		
2,556	need proof of	
SS		
MS		

2,557	unprecedented move	
SS		
MS		
2,558	blindly retaliating	
SS		
MS		
2,559	blind retaliation	
SS		
MS		
2,560	months of investigation	
SS		
MS		
2,561	a firm deadline	
SS		
MS		
2,562	false accusations	
SS		
MS		

2,563	raising questions	
SS		
MS		
2,564	unheard of	
SS		
MS		
2,565	treated fairly	
SS		
MS		
2,566	delayed another week	
SS		
MS		
2,567	supposed to	
SS		
MS		
2,568	a big hoax	
SS		
MS		

2,569	have faith in	
SS		
MS		
2,570	fully recognize	
SS		
MS		
2,571	has evaporated	
SS		
MS		
2,572	floated as a possibility	
SS		
MS		
2,573	rule nothing out	
SS		
MS		
2,574	not normal	
SS		
MS		

2,575	in plain sight	
SS		
MS		
2,576	one of the many	
SS		
MS		
2,577	under fire for	
SS		
MS		
2,578	a little hurt	
SS		
MS		
2,579	face backlash	
SS		
MS		
2,580	the appropriate response	
SS		
MS		

2,581	a very profound statement	
SS		
MS		
2,582	abuse of power	
SS		
MS		
2,583	jump on board	
SS		
MS		
2,584	dislike a number of	
SS		
MS		
2,585	clearly trying to	
SS		
MS		
2,586	come out with	
SS		
MS		

2,587	detrimental to	
SS		
MS		
2,588	do what it takes	
SS		
MS		
2,589	give an ultimatum	
SS		
MS		
2,590	a little rugged	
SS		
MS		
2,591	a positive influence	
SS		
MS		
2,592	interviewed by	
SS		
MS		

2,593	refuse to be rushed into	
SS		
MS		
2,594	confide in	
SS		
MS		
2,595	didn't sit right	
SS		
MS		
2,596	let it be known that	
SS		
MS		
2,597	very particular with	
SS		
MS		
2,598	lying to	
SS		
MS		

2,599	seasoned at	
SS		
MS		
2,600	the most outrageous requirement	
SS		
MS		
2,601	a couple of	
SS		
MS		
2,602	run into	
SS		
MS		
2,603	primary problem	
SS		
MS		
2,604	have a lot going	
SS		
MS		

2,605	very well received	
SS		
MS		
2,606	interfere in	
SS		
MS		
2,607	less eager to	
SS		
MS		
2,608	follow suit	
SS		
MS		
2,609	clash over	
SS		
MS		
2,610	sow discord among	
SS		
MS		

2,611	continue to worsen	
SS		
MS		
2,612	in the case of	
SS		
MS		
2,613	not at liberty to	
SS		
MS		
2,614	affiliated with	
SS		
MS		
2,615	push for	
SS		
MS		
2,616	bad for	
SS		
MS		

2,617	issued a denial	
SS		
MS		
2,618	absolutely right about	
SS		
MS		
2,619	in serious danger of	
SS		
MS		
2,620	deny any knowledge of	
SS		
MS		
2,621	in the interest of fairness	
SS		
MS		
2,622	be more specific	
SS		
MS		

2,623	make direct contact	
SS		
MS		
2,624	upside down	
SS		
MS		
2,625	immune to	
SS		
MS		
2,626	as an example	
SS		
MS		
2,627	go down the tubes	
SS		
MS		
2,628	jump to conclusions	
SS		
MS		

2,629	behind closed doors	
SS		
MS		
2,630	both within and without	
SS		
MS		
2,631	pretty nervous	
SS		
MS		
2,632	have low expectations of	
SS		
MS		
2,633	side with	
SS		
MS		
2,634	turn (one's) back on	
SS		
MS		

2,635	strangest of all	
SS		
MS		
2,636	complain about	
SS		
MS		
2,637	suffer the consequences of	
SS		
MS		
2,638	make or break	
SS		
MS		
2,639	have a falling out	
SS		
MS		
2,640	capitalize on	
SS		
MS		

2,641	try to reassure (someone)	
SS		
MS		
2,642	well aware of	
SS		
MS		
2,643	on purpose	
SS		
MS		
2,644	strictly forbidden	
SS		
MS		
2,645	never had a doubt	
SS		
MS		
2,646	fiery speech	
SS		
MS		

2,647	it would be a disaster if	
SS		
MS		
2,648	either way	
SS		
MS		
2,649	how is it possible that	
SS		
MS		
2,650	direct attack	
SS		
MS		
2,651	ramble incoherently	
SS		
MS		
2,652	the most insane thing	
SS		
MS		

2,653	published in	
SS		
MS		
2,654	a year after	
SS		
MS		
2,655	really happen	
SS		
MS		
2,656	a very good moment for	
SS		
MS		
2,657	a lot like	
SS		
MS		
2,658	a practical joke	
SS		
MS		

2,659	not consistent with	
SS		
MS		
2,660	have close ties to	
SS		
MS		
2,661	not improper	
SS		
MS		
2,662	aghast at	
SS		
MS		
2,663	cannot get past the fact that	
SS		
MS		
2,664	never mind that	
SS		
MS		

2,665	uttered by	
SS		
MS		
2,666	have normal relations with	
SS		
MS		
2,667	perfectly appropriate	
SS		
MS		
2,668	from the beginning	
SS		
MS		
2,669	top echelons	
SS		
MS		
2,670	in retrospect	
SS		
MS		

2,671	the best evidence	
SS		
MS		
2,672	the unavailability of	
SS		
MS		
2,673	prominent critics of	
SS		
MS		
2,674	more receptive to	
SS		
MS		
2,675	depends on who	
SS		
MS		
2,676	sense skepticism	
SS		
MS		

2,677	bow to pressure	
SS		
MS		
2,678	the same information	
SS		
MS		
2,679	so solicitous to	
SS		
MS		
2,680	so upset about	
SS		
MS		
2,681	get along with	
SS		
MS		
2,682	is/was deep distrust	
SS		
MS		

2,683	issued a rebuke	
SS		
MS		
2,684	akin to	
SS		
MS		
2,685	make a mistake	
SS		
MS		
2,686	speak against	
SS		
MS		
2,687	never doubting	
SS		
MS		
2,688	fight back tears	
SS		
MS		

2,689	a reasonable explanation	
SS		
MS		
2,690	truly shocking indeed	
SS		
MS		
2,691	not rule out	
SS		
MS		
2,692	must be exhausted	
SS		
MS		
2,693	found intriguing	
SS		
MS		
2,694	make an about face	
SS		
MS		

2,695	squeal on	
SS		
MS		
2,696	aim to achieve	
SS		
MS		
2,697	completely shocking	
SS		
MS		
2,698	has no plan	
SS		
MS		
2,699	serious intervention	
SS		
MS		
2,700	am/is/was totally cognizant of	
SS		
MS		

2,701	publicly embarrassing	
SS		
MS		
2,702	offer significant evidence	
SS		
MS		
2,703	show little appetite for	
SS		
MS		
2,704	totally prepared	
SS		
MS		
2,705	try to sift through	
SS		
MS		
2,706	a central theme	
SS		
MS		

2,707	an early victory	
SS		
MS		
2,708	there are no signs that	
SS		
MS		
2,709	don't think that	
SS		
MS		
2,710	publicly announced	
SS		
MS		
2,711	make progress	
SS		
MS		
2,712	months after	
SS		
MS		

2,713	punch above one's weight	
SS		
MS		
2,714	resigned over	
SS		
MS		
2,715	know the taste of defeat	
SS		
MS		
2,716	understand the mindset	
SS		
MS		
2,717	filter out	
SS		
MS		
2,718	almost proven	
SS		
MS		

2,719	rely on	
SS		
MS		
2,720	take a close look at	
SS		
MS		
2,721	hate the fact that	
SS		
MS		
2,722	still trying to figure out	
SS		
MS		
2,723	gotten more than	
SS		
MS		
2,724	a sobering reminder of	
SS		
MS		

2,725	rather uneasy feeling	
SS		
MS		
2,726	in the days after	
SS		
MS		
2,727	if approved	
SS		
MS		
2,728	scale back	
SS		
MS		
2,729	warned that	
SS		
MS		
2,730	it is inevitable that	
SS		
MS		

2,731	remain in the hunt	
SS		
MS		
2,732	go head to head with	
SS		
MS		
2,733	disappointing outcome	
SS		
MS		
2,734	on high alert	
SS		
MS		
2,735	many ordinary people	
SS		
MS		
2,736	breach security	
SS		
MS		

2,737	cannot confirm	
SS		
MS		
2,738	few and far between	
SS		
MS		
2,739	one of the successes	
SS		
MS		
2,740	extend an olive branch to	
SS		
MS		
2,741	no personal issue with	
SS		
MS		
2,742	enforce laws	
SS		
MS		

2,743	have a contentious exchange	
SS		
MS		
2,744	has the courage to	
SS		
MS		
2,745	nothing (one) had expected	
SS		
MS		
2,746	turn out to be	
SS		
MS		
2,747	remember thinking	
SS		
MS		
2,748	asked to read	
SS		
MS		

2,749	have no idea	
SS		
MS		
2,750	seem possible	
SS		
MS		
2,751	seemed promising	
SS		
MS		
2,752	go back to	
SS		
MS		
2,753	fly into	
SS		
MS		
2,754	book promotion	
SS		
MS		

2,755	based on	
SS		
MS		
2,756	fixed opinion	
SS		
MS		
2,757	do business as usual	
SS		
MS		
2,758	start talking	
SS		
MS		
2,759	understand that	
SS		
MS		
2,760	how limiting X can be	
SS		
MS		

2,761	it's often harder for	
SS		
MS		
2,762	denied knowing	
SS		
MS		
2,763	completely at odds with	
SS		
MS		
2,764	acquiescence to	
SS		
MS		
2,765	urgent need	
SS		
MS		
2,766	make connections with	
SS		
MS		

2,767	recognize that	
SS		
MS		
2,768	an encounter with	
SS		
MS		
2,769	give rise to	
SS		
MS		
2,770	an honest study of	
SS		
MS		
2,771	foist (something) on	
SS		
MS		
2,772	seem bizarre	
SS		
MS		

2,773	spell the end of	
SS		
MS		
2,774	most in need	
SS		
MS		
2,775	at the precise moment	
SS		
MS		
2,776	conveniently forget	
SS		
MS		
2,777	historical ignorance	
SS		
MS		
2,778	cooperation with	
SS		
MS		

2,779	make a contribution	
SS		
MS		
2,780	highly-rated	
SS		
MS		
2,781	don't know how long	
SS		
MS		
2,782	could have done more	
SS		
MS		
2,783	exclusive list	
SS		
MS		
2,784	make an educated guess	
SS		
MS		

2,785	an appropriate time	
SS		
MS		
2,786	on the grounds that	
SS		
MS		
2,787	demand that	
SS		
MS		
2,788	reduced to	
SS		
MS		
2,789	had not expected	
SS		
MS		
2,790	still talking about	
SS		
MS		

2,791	should be careful not to	
SS		
MS		
2,792	gamble on	
SS		
MS		
2,793	completely oblivious to	
SS		
MS		
2,794	live in luxury	
SS		
MS		
2,795	decided not to	
SS		
MS		
2,796	shall decide	
SS		
MS		

2,797	entirely up to	
SS		
MS		
2,798	seem bizarre	
SS		
MS		
2,799	spell the end of	
SS		
MS		
2,800	a few days later	
SS		
MS		
2,801	coexistence between A and B	
SS		
MS		
2,802	could be counted on	
SS		
MS		

2,803	persist in	
SS		
MS		
2,804	replaced by	
SS		
MS		
2,805	subjected to	
SS		
MS		
2,806	resign over	
SS		
MS		
2,807	cancel out	
SS		
MS		
2,808	a growing number of	
SS		
MS		

2,809	could be useful	
SS		
MS		
2,810	harbor resentment	
SS		
MS		
2,811	open season on	
SS		
MS		
2,812	accused of	
SS		
MS		
2,813	help X understand	
SS		
MS		
2,814	is/was guilty of	
SS		
MS		

2,815	almost no one	
SS		
MS		
2,816	continue to pretend	
SS		
MS		
2,817	tend to believe that	
SS		
MS		
2,818	desperately want	
SS		
MS		
2,819	centered on	
SS		
MS		
2,820	mounting sense of dread	
SS		
MS		

2,821	it's hard to see	
SS		
MS		
2,822	heading for	
SS		
MS		
2,823	almost exactly	
SS		
MS		
2,824	possible not to	
SS		
MS		
2,825	come in waves	
SS		
MS		
2,826	brought down by	
SS		
MS		

2,827	inquiry into	
SS		
MS		
2,828	serve to	
SS		
MS		
2,829	plunge into	
SS		
MS		
2,830	extremely fragile	
SS		
MS		
2,831	early on	
SS		
MS		
2,832	actively working with	
SS		
MS		

2,833	explain again	
SS		
MS		
2,834	incredibly demanding	
SS		
MS		
2,835	a large range of	
SS		
MS		
2,836	raise worries about	
SS		
MS		
2,837	raise concerns about	
SS		
MS		
2,838	nothing short of	
SS		
MS		

2,839	pay lip service to	
SS		
MS		
2,840	whether real or perceived	
SS		
MS		
2,841	ramp up	
SS		
MS		
2,842	in the wake of	
SS		
MS		
2,843	ingratiate (oneself) with	
SS		
MS		
2,844	get things wrong	
SS		
MS		

2,845	heated debate about	
SS		
MS		
2,846	a memorial for	
SS		
MS		
2,847	a bit surprised by	
SS		
MS		
2,848	completely inappropriate	
SS		
MS		
2,849	commensurate with	
SS		
MS		
2,850	range of possibilities	
SS		
MS		

2,851	opportunities that await	
SS		
MS		
2,852	called upon to	
SS		
MS		
2,853	on behalf of	
SS		
MS		
2,854	fight against	
SS		
MS		
2,855	equality of opportunity	
SS		
MS		
2,856	hard to know	
SS		
MS		

2,857	encouraged by	
SS		
MS		
2,858	it so happened that	
SS		
MS		
2,859	seem extraordinary	
SS		
MS		
2,860	coincided with	
SS		
MS		
2,861	stress the importance of	
SS		
MS		
2,862	struggle with	
SS		
MS		

2,863	strongly influenced by	
SS		
MS		
2,864	make use of	
SS		
MS		
2,865	how much time	
SS		
MS		
2,866	trained to	
SS		
MS		
2,867	relate a story to	
SS		
MS		
2,868	once you have	
SS		
MS		

2,869	demonstrate that	
SS		
MS		
2,870	give guidance to	
SS		
MS		
2,871	the problems inherent in	
SS		
MS		
2,872	that doesn't begin to capture	
SS		
MS		
2,873	charm offensive	
SS		
MS		
2,874	before and during the	
SS		
MS		

2,875	try to halt a slide in popularity of	
SS		
MS		
2,876	kid gloves	
SS		
MS		
2,877	more likely	
SS		
MS		
2,878	euphoria at	
SS		
MS		
2,879	celebrate victory	
SS		
MS		
2,880	health emergency	
SS		
MS		

2,881	background check	
SS		
MS		
2,882	pet project	
SS		
MS		
2,883	because of the profusion of	
SS		
MS		
2,884	reduce (one's) efforts	
SS		
MS		
2,885	practical education	
SS		
MS		
2,886	share concerns about	
SS		
MS		

2,887	go the extra mile	
SS		
MS		
2,888	absolute right question	
SS		
MS		
2,889	rip up	
SS		
MS		
2,890	led me to believe that	
SS		
MS		
2,891	could not be stopped	
SS		
MS		
2,892	caution against	
SS		
MS		

2,893	ended up	
SS		
MS		
2,894	denial of	
SS		
MS		
2,895	going back and forth	
SS		
MS		
2,896	come out of the blue	
SS		
MS		
2,897	have evidence of	
SS		
MS		
2,898	scream at the top of (one's) lungs	
SS		
MS		

2,899	it is possible that	
SS		
MS		
2,900	an error	
SS		
MS		
2,901	lauded for	
SS		
MS		
2,902	prefer to go by	
SS		
MS		
2,903	allegations of	
SS		
MS		
2,904	pose a question	
SS		
MS		

2,905	step down	
SS		
MS		
2,906	highly unusual	
SS		
MS		
2,907	a hush agreement	
SS		
MS		
2,908	seek records	
SS		
MS		
2,909	prevent (one) from	
SS		
MS		
2,910	on condition of anonymity	
SS		
MS		

2,911	decide whether	
SS		
MS		
2,912	will meet	
SS		
MS		
2,913	make an appearance	
SS		
MS		
2,914	send back	
SS		
MS		
2,915	wasn't worried about	
SS		
MS		
2,916	know the pain of	
SS		
MS		

2,917	yearn to	
SS		
MS		
2,918	beg for	
SS		
MS		
2,919	grounds for	
SS		
MS		
2,920	seek refuge in	
SS		
MS		
2,921	hold back tears	
SS		
MS		
2,922	trapped in	
SS		
MS		

2,923	in custody	
SS		
MS		
2,924	hold on to	
SS		
MS		
2,925	pave the way for	
SS		
MS		
2,926	it takes work for	
SS		
MS		
2,927	not a given	
SS		
MS		
2,928	unlikely to be	
SS		
MS		

2,929	all the more desperate to	
SS		
MS		
2,930	squeak through	
SS		
MS		
2,931	reminded of	
SS		
MS		
2,932	ill equipped for	
SS		
MS		
2,933	not refuted	
SS		
MS		
2,934	in chaos	
SS		
MS		

2,935	X is key to	
SS		
MS		
2,936	toggle between A and B	
SS		
MS		
2,937	flock to	
SS		
MS		
2,938	there's no question that	
SS		
MS		
2,939	even less interesting	
SS		
MS		
2,940	wreak havoc on	
SS		
MS		

2,941	time and again	
SS		
MS		
2,942	reminded of	
SS		
MS		
2,943	for (one's) efforts	
SS		
MS		
2,944	beef up	
SS		
MS		
2,945	snuff out	
SS		
MS		
2,946	respect the idea of	
SS		
MS		

2,947	build on	
SS		
MS		
2,948	venture ever deeper into	
SS		
MS		
2,949	willing to speak	
SS		
MS		
2,950	not so long ago	
SS		
MS		
2,951	public outcry	
SS		
MS		
2,952	in an effort to	
SS		
MS		

2,953	an impediment to	
SS		
MS		
2,954	stress that	
SS		
MS		
2,955	unwillingness to	
SS		
MS		
2,956	provided by	
SS		
MS		
2,957	for the second time	
SS		
MS		
2,958	want to be able to	
SS		
MS		

2,959	petition for	
SS		
MS		
2,960	organized around	
SS		
MS		
2,961	become more common	
SS		
MS		
2,962	seen sharper increases	
SS		
MS		
2,963	in recent years	
SS		
MS		
2,964	the sole means of	
SS		
MS		

2,965	an axe to grind	
SS		
MS		
2,966	struck by	
SS		
MS		
2,967	badly need	
SS		
MS		
2,968	risk danger	
SS		
MS		
2,969	accustomed to	
SS		
MS		
2,970	surprised at	
SS		
MS		

2,971	similar to	
SS		
MS		
2,972	a visit to	
SS		
MS		
2,973	offer commentary on	
SS		
MS		
2,974	not ideal	
SS		
MS		
2,975	poke fun at	
SS		
MS		
2,976	speak with	
SS		
MS		

2,977	at the height of	
SS		
MS		
2,978	draw stinging criticism	
SS		
MS		
2,979	fueled by	
SS		
MS		
2,980	have reason to think that	
SS		
MS		
2,981	in order to feel	
SS		
MS		
2,982	search for	
SS		
MS		

2,983	identify with	
SS		
MS		
2,984	feel a strong sense of	
SS		
MS		
2,985	a worrisome development	
SS		
MS		
2,986	really awful	
SS		
MS		
2,987	stave off	
SS		
MS		
2,988	make contributions to	
SS		
MS		

2,989	one by one	
SS		
MS		
2,990	engage in	
SS		
MS		
2,991	understand that	
SS		
MS		
2,992	not able to maintain	
SS		
MS		
2,993	best able to cope with	
SS		
MS		
2,994	linked to	
SS		
MS		

2,995	gone off the rails	
SS		
MS		
2,996	worth saving	
SS		
MS		
2,997	encouraging of	
SS		
MS		
2,998	back down	
SS		
MS		
2,999	in an attempt to	
SS		
MS		
3,000	very rarely see	
SS		
MS		

3,001	entertain the notion that	
SS		
MS		
3,002	got raked over the coals	
SS		
MS		
3,003	it's a mistake to	
SS		
MS		
3,004	pay a price for	
SS		
MS		
3,005	contend with	
SS		
MS		
3,006	undertaken by	
SS		
MS		

3,007	upon further consideration	
SS		
MS		
3,008	a trip like no other	
SS		
MS		
3,009	glowing reports	
SS		
MS		
3,010	board a flight	
SS		
MS		
3,011	long-lasting effects	
SS		
MS		
3,012	feel guilty	
SS		
MS		

3,013	to one's credit	
SS		
MS		
3,014	physically remove (someone)	
SS		
MS		
3,015	freak out	
SS		
MS		
3,016	prepare for	
SS		
MS		
3,017	no clear plan	
SS		
MS		
3,018	split up	
SS		
MS		

3,019	just got back from	
SS		
MS		
3,020	an uncomfortable position	
SS		
MS		
3,021	clean up	
SS		
MS		
3,022	take a weird turn	
SS		
MS		
3,023	for the record	
SS		
MS		
3,024	a mock interview	
SS		
MS		

3,025	had to respond to	
SS		
MS		
3,026	eerily reminiscent of	
SS		
MS		
3,027	cannot believe	
SS		
MS		
3,028	just the other day	
SS		
MS		
3,029	hold out for	
SS		
MS		
3,030	want to undo	
SS		
MS		

3,031	attempt to	
SS		
MS		
3,032	once again	
SS		
MS		
3,033	beyond belief	
SS		
MS		
3,034	the most explosive	
SS		
MS		
3,035	did not need	
SS		
MS		
3,036	distant from	
SS		
MS		

3,037	what is amazing is that	
SS		
MS		
3,038	so lucky that	
SS		
MS		
3,039	more pronounced	
SS		
MS		
3,040	of sound mind	
SS		
MS		
3,041	a prudent strategy	
SS		
MS		
3,042	quite shocking	
SS		
MS		

3,043	avoidance of	
SS		
MS		
3,044	scary looking	
SS		
MS		
3,045	on the strength of	
SS		
MS		
3,046	own up to	
SS		
MS		
3,047	a genuine threat	
SS		
MS		
3,048	influx of	
SS		
MS		

3,049	take up the slack	
SS		
MS		
3,050	with no plan for	
SS		
MS		
3,051	did not bother to	
SS		
MS		
3,052	what this means is that	
SS		
MS		
3,053	is/was sure about	
SS		
MS		
3,054	did herself no favours	
SS		
MS		

3,055	appeared to indicate	
SS		
MS		
3,056	the first indication	
SS		
MS		
3,057	duration of	
SS		
MS		
3,058	provide basic training	
SS		
MS		
3,059	an urgent request	
SS		
MS		
3,060	have knowledge of	
SS		
MS		

3,061	peripherally involved	
SS		
MS		
3,062	at the point	
SS		
MS		
3,063	want no part of	
SS		
MS		
3,064	in deep conflict with	
SS		
MS		
3,065	newly implemented	
SS		
MS		
3,066	pride (oneself) on	
SS		
MS		

3,067	have no desire to	
SS		
MS		
3,068	it seems unclear what	
SS		
MS		
3,069	extremely disappointed	
SS		
MS		
3,070	reunited with	
SS		
MS		
3,071	not going to be a part of	
SS		
MS		
3,072	separated from	
SS		
MS		

3,073	unwitting role in	
SS		
MS		
3,074	inescapable fact	
SS		
MS		
3,075	after midnight	
SS		
MS		
3,076	nevertheless choose to	
SS		
MS		
3,077	a secret too big to be kept	
SS		
MS		
3,078	grant anonymity	
SS		
MS		

3,079	started a fight with	
SS		
MS		
3,080	not authorized to	
SS		
MS		
3,081	for about a month	
SS		
MS		
3,082	taken away from	
SS		
MS		
3,083	in coming days	
SS		
MS		
3,084	up and running	
SS		
MS		

3,085	specifically for	
SS		
MS		
3,086	since found out	
SS		
MS		
3,087	this past week	
SS		
MS		
3,088	on the border	
SS		
MS		
3,089	first thing in the morning	
SS		
MS		
3,090	converge on	
SS		
MS		

3,091	there is no reason to think	
SS		
MS		
3,092	nothing better to do	
SS		
MS		
3,093	very happy to	
SS		
MS		
3,094	up to date	
SS		
MS		
3,095	in the face of	
SS		
MS		
3,096	the most trusted	
SS		
MS		

3,097	the ability to listen to	
SS		
MS		
3,098	show maturity	
SS		
MS		
3,099	shame on	
SS		
MS		
3,100	the memory of	
SS		
MS		
3,101	the long-term effects of	
SS		
MS		
3,102	the effect on	
SS		
MS		

3,103	the ultimate problem	
SS		
MS		
3,104	suffer for	
SS		
MS		
3,105	through no fault of (one's) own	
SS		
MS		
3,106	take X into account	
SS		
MS		
3,107	a wrong-headed approach	
SS		
MS		
3,108	draconian measures	
SS		
MS		

3,109	stand accused of	
SS		
MS		
3,110	take the risk	
SS		
MS		
3,111	miss out on	
SS		
MS		
3,112	do not recall	
SS		
MS		
3,113	a horror show	
SS		
MS		
3,114	vividly remember	
SS		
MS		

3,115	stand shoulder to shoulder with	
SS		
MS		
3,116	quick to	
SS		
MS		
3,117	put the spotlight on	
SS		
MS		
3,118	the latest salvo	
SS		
MS		
3,119	inured to	
SS		
MS		
3,120	offer a glimpse of	
SS		
MS		

3,121	awestruck by	
SS		
MS		
3,122	when push comes to shove	
SS		
MS		
3,123	dispense with	
SS		
MS		
3,124	nothing to lose	
SS		
MS		
3,125	got fed up	
SS		
MS		
3,126	almost unbearable	
SS		
MS		

3,127	bear down on	
SS		
MS		
3,128	unacceptable behaviour	
SS		
MS		
3,129	excellent at	
SS		
MS		
3,130	less shocking	
SS		
MS		
3,131	seem uncertain of	
SS		
MS		
3,132	at the core	
SS		
MS		

3,133	absolutely terrific	
SS		
MS		
3,134	extremely enjoyable	
SS		
MS		
3,135	almost always revealing	
SS		
MS		
3,136	fixated on	
SS		
MS		
3,137	best known for	
SS		
MS		
3,138	respond immediately	
SS		
MS		

3,139	look ahead	
SS		
MS		
3,140	having none of it	
SS		
MS		
3,141	under fire	
SS		
MS		
3,142	calls to resign	
SS		
MS		
3,143	immersed in	
SS		
MS		
3,144	gaze upon	
SS		
MS		

3,145	in the final months of	
SS		
MS		
3,146	at all costs	
SS		
MS		
3,147	run headlong into	
SS		
MS		
3,148	a fairly standard practice	
SS		
MS		
3,149	very conscientiously	
SS		
MS		
3,150	the last thing you want to do	
SS		
MS		

3,151	sheer lack of	
SS		
MS		
3,152	not have much of a sense of	
SS		
MS		
3,153	fortunate to have	
SS		
MS		
3,154	fully support	
SS		
MS		
3,155	cringe at the thought of	
SS		
MS		
3,156	an option for	
SS		
MS		

3,157	dreaded by	
SS		
MS		
3,158	in full swing	
SS		
MS		
3,159	in search of	
SS		
MS		
3,160	the threat of	
SS		
MS		
3,161	complicit in	
SS		
MS		
3,162	feel less alone	
SS		
MS		

3,163	threaten to topple	
SS		
MS		
3,164	the effect of	
SS		
MS		
3,165	so stark	
SS		
MS		
3,166	in disbelief	
SS		
MS		
3,167	wonder if	
SS		
MS		
3,168	in the early stages of	
SS		
MS		

3,169	shore up	
SS		
MS		
3,170	unable to come to any agreement on	
SS		
MS		
3,171	it is impossible to tell	
SS		
MS		
3,172	utterly bewildered by	
SS		
MS		
3,173	a bone of contention	
SS		
MS		
3,174	with delight	
SS		
MS		

3,175	it can often feel like	
SS		
MS		
3,176	move as swiftly as possible	
SS		
MS		
3,177	the challenge for	
SS		
MS		
3,178	dare to get involved in	
SS		
MS		
3,179	minimize the impact of	
SS		
MS		
3,180	the most important piece of	
SS		
MS		

3,181	could not resist	
SS		
MS		
3,182	going too far	
SS		
MS		
3,183	mentioned by	
SS		
MS		
3,184	deeply moved	
SS		
MS		
3,185	fair use of	
SS		
MS		
3,186	vital to	
SS		
MS		

3,187	seething over	
SS		
MS		
3,188	there's nothing wrong with	
SS		
MS		
3,189	nobody needs to	
SS		
MS		
3,190	interfere with	
SS		
MS		
3,191	quite generous	
SS		
MS		
3,192	stomp on	
SS		
MS		

3,193	escape the temptation to	
SS		
MS		
3,194	booted off	
SS		
MS		
3,195	made comments about	
SS		
MS		
3,196	not doing as well as	
SS		
MS		
3,197	much more aggressive	
SS		
MS		
3,198	a series of	
SS		
MS		

3,199	call for an apology	
SS		
MS		
3,200	get consensus on	
SS		
MS		
3,201	a significant acknowledgement	
SS		
MS		
3,202	deadly decision	
SS		
MS		
3,203	trying to understand	
SS		
MS		
3,204	figure out how to	
SS		
MS		

3,205	make no mistake	
SS		
MS		
3,206	do not abide by	
SS		
MS		
3,207	received a dressing down	
SS		
MS		
3,208	fact-check (someone)	
SS		
MS		
3,209	a fast-growing problem	
SS		
MS		
3,210	dig in	
SS		
MS		

3,211	walk (someone) through something	
SS		
MS		
3,212	what's infuriating is	
SS		
MS		
3,213	shameful beyond description	
SS		
MS		
3,214	the one bright spot in X is	
SS		
MS		
3,215	over the last (X) years	
SS		
MS		
3,216	can't figure out what to do	
SS		
MS		

3,217	more welcoming of	
SS		
MS		
3,218	more humane	
SS		
MS		
3,219	mostly care about	
SS		
MS		
3,220	a defining moment	
SS		
MS		
3,221	total chaos	
SS		
MS		
3,222	horrific situation	
SS		
MS		

3,223	start anew	
SS		
MS		
3,224	obvious to	
SS		
MS		
3,225	cannot be trusted	
SS		
MS		
3,226	have empathy for	
SS		
MS		
3,227	foisted on	
SS		
MS		
3,228	enforce the law	
SS		
MS		

3,229	largely accurate	
SS		
MS		
3,230	vocal about	
SS		
MS		
3,231	battle with	
SS		
MS		
3,232	disproportionately represented	
SS		
MS		
3,233	convince myself that	
SS		
MS		
3,234	worthy enough	
SS		
MS		

3,235	have in common	
SS		
MS		
3,236	what is acceptable	
SS		
MS		
3,237	become interested in	
SS		
MS		
3,238	the rise of	
SS		
MS		
3,239	point to	
SS		
MS		
3,240	have a sizable role	
SS		
MS		

3,241	fail to understand	
SS		
MS		
3,242	there is no proven method	
SS		
MS		
3,243	it is crucial that	
SS		
MS		
3,244	willing to collaborate with	
SS		
MS		
3,245	hesitate to	
SS		
MS		
3,246	switch from	
SS		
MS		

3,247	opt to	
SS		
MS		
3,248	geared towards	
SS		
MS		
3,249	contrary to	
SS		
MS		
3,250	fearful of	
SS		
MS		
3,251	turn against	
SS		
MS		
3,252	one of the most fascinating	
SS		
MS		

3,253	to my knowledge	
SS		
MS		
3,254	move away from	
SS		
MS		
3,255	aspire to	
SS		
MS		
3,256	thrive on	
SS		
MS		
3,257	to better understand	
SS		
MS		
3,258	inspired to	
SS		
MS		

3,259	so far ahead of	
SS		
MS		
3,260	equally important is	
SS		
MS		
3,261	have control over	
SS		
MS		
3,262	speculate that	
SS		
MS		
3,263	compensate for	
SS		
MS		
3,264	raise questions about	
SS		
MS		

3,265	it is no coincidence that	
SS		
MS		
3,266	emphasize that	
SS		
MS		
3,267	it is unclear what will happen to	
SS		
MS		
3,268	organized by	
SS		
MS		
3,269	the advent of	
SS		
MS		
3,270	enthralled with	
SS		
MS		

3,271	head over to	
SS		
MS		
3,272	consistently show that	
SS		
MS		
3,273	a far cry from	
SS		
MS		
3,274	mean little	
SS		
MS		
3,275	number of deals	
SS		
MS		
3,276	significant takeaway	
SS		
MS		

3,277	wonder why	
SS		
MS		
3,278	did research on	
SS		
MS		
3,279	much to the chagrin of	
SS		
MS		
3,280	gain knowledge about	
SS		
MS		
3,281	feel doubtful	
SS		
MS		
3,282	explicit about	
SS		
MS		

3,283	make compromises	
SS		
MS		
3,284	lack of clarity about	
SS		
MS		
3,285	confused about	
SS		
MS		
3,286	the entire time	
SS		
MS		
3,287	miss out	
SS		
MS		
3,288	overruled by	
SS		
MS		

3,289	never understand	
SS		
MS		
3,290	essential for	
SS		
MS		
3,291	have good sense	
SS		
MS		
3,292	seek consensus on	
SS		
MS		
3,293	accustomed to	
SS		
MS		
3,294	caught my attention	
SS		
MS		

3,295	crucial for	
SS		
MS		
3,296	the most important decision	
SS		
MS		
3,297	take better advantage of	
SS		
MS		
3,298	strike the right balance	
SS		
MS		
3,299	avoid becoming	
SS		
MS		
3,300	have no obligation to	
SS		
MS		

3,301	consulted about	
SS		
MS		
3,302	the most effective	
SS		
MS		
3,303	take too long to	
SS		
MS		
3,304	ultimate responsibility for	
SS		
MS		
3,305	become familiar with	
SS		
MS		
3,306	wrestle over	
SS		
MS		

3,307	respected for	
SS		
MS		
3,308	the best way to	
SS		
MS		
3,309	the result of	
SS		
MS		
3,310	really influential	
SS		
MS		
3,311	ready to	
SS		
MS		
3,312	the only way that	
SS		
MS		

3,313	get really good at	
SS		
MS		
3,314	get excited about	
SS		
MS		
3,315	it is less tenable than ever to	
SS		
MS		
3,316	the sticking point	
SS		
MS		
3,317	projected to	
SS		
MS		
3,318	invest in	
SS		
MS		

3,319	on more than one occasion	
SS		
MS		
3,320	agree to	
SS		
MS		
3,321	come up with ways to	
SS		
MS		
3,322	unfairly criticized by	
SS		
MS		
3,323	have no regrets about	
SS		
MS		
3,324	increase risk for	
SS		
MS		

3,325	lack of access to	
SS		
MS		
3,326	never been afraid to	
SS		
MS		
3,327	prefer to do	
SS		
MS		
3,328	spend more time with	
SS		
MS		
3,329	leading to	
SS		
MS		
3,330	cannot assume that	
SS		
MS		

3,331	well underway	
SS		
MS		
3,332	likely to resort to	
SS		
MS		
3,333	associated with	
SS		
MS		
3,334	with great difficulty	
SS		
MS		
3,335	not a zero-sum game	
SS		
MS		
3,336	less likely to	
SS		
MS		

3,337	set up as	
SS		
MS		
3,338	accrue to	
SS		
MS		
3,339	push the boundaries	
SS		
MS		
3,340	greatly influence	
SS		
MS		
3,341	at an unprecedented rate	
SS		
MS		
3,342	how the facts unfold	
SS		
MS		

3,343	as it turns out	
SS		
MS		
3,344	start seeing	
SS		
MS		
3,345	fly off the handle	
SS		
MS		
3,346	high on	
SS		
MS		
3,347	embark on	
SS		
MS		
3,348	distracted by	
SS		
MS		

3,349	disengage from	
SS		
MS		
3,350	blissfully unaware of	
SS		
MS		
3,351	however much	
SS		
MS		
3,352	reveal that	
SS		
MS		
3,353	just to be clear	
SS		
MS		
3,354	an intractable problem	
SS		
MS		

3,355	chances are	
SS		
MS		
3,356	get worked up	
SS		
MS		
3,357	make unreasonable demands	
SS		
MS		
3,358	limits to	
SS		
MS		
3,359	keep up	
SS		
MS		
3,360	can't stress enough	
SS		
MS		

3,361	rise through the ranks	
SS		
MS		
3,362	take the helm	
SS		
MS		
3,363	partnership with	
SS		
MS		
3,364	commitment to	
SS		
MS		
3,365	about to tackle	
SS		
MS		
3,366	gravitate to	
SS		
MS		

3,367	a compelling story	
SS		
MS		
3,368	another component	
SS		
MS		
3,369	really come to life	
SS		
MS		
3,370	isn't going to cut it	
SS		
MS		
3,371	acclaimed as	
SS		
MS		
3,372	generous to	
SS		
MS		

3,373	reputation for	
SS		
MS		
3,374	onset of	
SS		
MS		
3,375	the bare minimum	
SS		
MS		
3,376	invaluable feedback	
SS		
MS		
3,377	fall into the category of	
SS		
MS		
3,378	blend in	
SS		
MS		

3,379	hold off on	
SS		
MS		
3,380	wary of	
SS		
MS		
3,381	feel bound to	
SS		
MS		
3,382	intersect with	
SS		
MS		
3,383	highly relevant	
SS		
MS		
3,384	at an all-time high	
SS		
MS		

3,385	leave (something/someone) by the wayside	
SS		
MS		
3,386	bank on	
SS		
MS		
3,387	swayed by	
SS		
MS		
3,388	not afraid to	
SS		
MS		
3,389	turn on the nightly news	
SS		
MS		
3,390	off to a strong start	
SS		
MS		

3,391	go above and beyond	
SS		
MS		
3,392	with impunity	
SS		
MS		
3,393	get (something) off the ground	
SS		
MS		
3,394	downright negative	
SS		
MS		
3,395	make a quick buck	
SS		
MS		
3,396	do a double take	
SS		
MS		

3,397	reflect on	
SS		
MS		
3,398	can come off as	
SS		
MS		
3,399	substantially easier	
SS		
MS		
3,400	grateful to	
SS		
MS		
3,401	increase the likelihood that	
SS		
MS		
3,402	add fuel to the fire	
SS		
MS		

3,403	purport to	
SS		
MS		
3,404	in need of assistance	
SS		
MS		
3,405	lend a hand to	
SS		
MS		
3,406	time and time again	
SS		
MS		
3,407	return a favor	
SS		
MS		
3,408	partake in	
SS		
MS		

3,409	come up with	
SS		
MS		
3,410	tap into	
SS		
MS		
3,411	make a bold prediction	
SS		
MS		
3,412	a handful of	
SS		
MS		
3,413	unique perspective	
SS		
MS		
3,414	security clearance	
SS		
MS		

3,415	master the details of	
SS		
MS		
3,416	a side point	
SS		
MS		
3,417	make one's bones with	
SS		
MS		
3,418	unlimited power	
SS		
MS		
3,419	find evidence of	
SS		
MS		
3,420	play into the hands of	
SS		
MS		

3,421	sing like a canary	
SS		
MS		
3,422	get the benefit of	
SS		
MS		
3,423	entitled to	
SS		
MS		
3,424	in this vicinity	
SS		
MS		
3,425	likes the sound of his own voice	
SS		
MS		
3,426	out of personal funds	
SS		
MS		

3,427	off the cuff	
SS		
MS		
3,428	push back on	
SS		
MS		
3,429	open another door	
SS		
MS		
3,430	top-tier lawyers	
SS		
MS		
3,431	take the fifth	
SS		
MS		
3,432	with a great deal of trepidation	
SS		
MS		

3,433	in the hunt for	
SS		
MS		
3,434	thumb one's nose at someone/something	
SS		
MS		
3,435	lob accusations at/towards someone	
SS		
MS		
3,436	a portion of the time	
SS		
MS		
3,437	it took a minute	
SS		
MS		
3,438	distraught by	
SS		
MS		

3,439	doesn't hold water	
SS		
MS		
3,440	leap to conclusions	
SS		
MS		
3,441	on the basis of	
SS		
MS		
3,442	retrieve from	
SS		
MS		
3,443	give free rein to	
SS		
MS		
3,444	survive and even thrive	
SS		
MS		

3,445	take one's lumps	
SS		
MS		
3,446	close in on	
SS		
MS		
3,447	start off	
SS		
MS		
3,448	be on the rebound	
SS		
MS		
3,449	as a function of	
SS		
MS		
3,450	mood swings	
SS		
MS		

3,451	full access to	
SS		
MS		
3,452	lose motivation	
SS		
MS		
3,453	domestic squabble	
SS		
MS		
3,454	from bad to worse	
SS		
MS		
3,455	shadowy business empire	
SS		
MS		
3,456	the age-old canard	
SS		
MS		

3,457	cross the line	
SS		
MS		
3,458	an urgent response	
SS		
MS		
3,459	followed almost immediately by	
SS		
MS		
3,460	back in someone's good graces	
SS		
MS		
3,461	an antidote to	
SS		
MS		
3,462	on a whim	
SS		
MS		

3,463	always ends up badly	
SS		
MS		
3,464	tend to prefer	
SS		
MS		
3,465	center around	
SS		
MS		
3,466	in the course of	
SS		
MS		
3,467	year in and year out	
SS		
MS		
3,468	slightly more than	
SS		
MS		

3,469	tune into	
SS		
MS		
3,470	where things stand	
SS		
MS		
3,471	untouched by	
SS		
MS		
3,472	without provocation	
SS		
MS		
3,473	a tough choice	
SS		
MS		
3,474	take for granted	
SS		
MS		

3,475	overlook contradictions	
SS		
MS		
3,476	grow restive about	
SS		
MS		
3,477	complicit with	
SS		
MS		
3,478	cater to	
SS		
MS		
3,479	in session	
SS		
MS		
3,480	cannot decide whether to	
SS		
MS		

3,481	under the impression that	
SS		
MS		
3,482	keep arguing about	
SS		
MS		
3,483	get grilled about	
SS		
MS		
3,484	on the off-chance that	
SS		
MS		
3,485	can't wait to	
SS		
MS		
3,486	with support from	
SS		
MS		

3,487	deep insights into	
SS		
MS		
3,488	major illusions about	
SS		
MS		
3,489	profoundly grateful for	
SS		
MS		
3,490	expected to be	
SS		
MS		
3,491	hamper creativity	
SS		
MS		
3,492	undue strain	
SS		
MS		

3,493	come at a personal cost	
SS		
MS		
3,494	hope to find	
SS		
MS		
3,495	hope to found	
SS		
MS		
3,496	divide (one's) time between A and B	
SS		
MS		
3,497	given over totally to	
SS		
MS		
3,498	maniacal dedication	
SS		
MS		

3,499	pass down from	
SS		
MS		
3,500	backbreaking task	
SS		
MS		
3,501	does not do things by halves	
SS		
MS		
3,502	vocal defender	
SS		
MS		
3,503	dismissive of	
SS		
MS		
3,504	flood the market with	
SS		
MS		

3,505	hesitant to	
SS		
MS		
3,506	step up	
SS		
MS		
3,507	labour intensive	
SS		
MS		
3,508	stand to lose	
SS		
MS		
3,509	eschew hard work	
SS		
MS		
3,510	rattled by	
SS		
MS		

3,511	look bleak	
SS		
MS		
3,512	best left to	
SS		
MS		
3,513	a supernatural feat	
SS		
MS		
3,514	imbued with	
SS		
MS		
3,515	in the blink of an eye	
SS		
MS		
3,516	blessed with	
SS		
MS		

3,517	obsessed with	
SS		
MS		
3,518	far from the only reason why	
SS		
MS		
3,519	crucial factor in	
SS		
MS		
3,520	shuttle back and forth between	
SS		
MS		
3,521	put off	
SS		
MS		
3,522	stand at	
SS		
MS		

3,523	friendly relations	
SS		
MS		
3,524	a glut of	
SS		
MS		
3,525	decline to	
SS		
MS		
3,526	turn (someone) down	
SS		
MS		
3,527	fear repercussions	
SS		
MS		
3,528	is terribly counter-productive	
SS		
MS		

3,529	overly optimistic	
SS		
MS		
3,530	risk retaliation from	
SS		
MS		
3,531	iron out differences	
SS		
MS		
3,532	envisage a time where	
SS		
MS		
3,533	seismic changes to	
SS		
MS		
3,534	dwindle to	
SS		
MS		

3,535	disappear completely	
SS		
MS		
3,536	a fraction of	
SS		
MS		
3,537	put (something) in jeopardy	
SS		
MS		
3,538	pose a challenge for	
SS		
MS		
3,539	carry on	
SS		
MS		
3,540	in response to	
SS		
MS		

3,541	steep cuts in	
SS		
MS		
3,542	vocal critic of	
SS		
MS		
3,543	make the ask	
SS		
MS		
3,544	culminate in	
SS		
MS		
3,545	a well-deserved reputation	
SS		
MS		
3,546	bounce back	
SS		
MS		

3,547	take hold	
SS		
MS		
3,548	bode well for	
SS		
MS		
3,549	anchored to	
SS		
MS		
3,550	surpass expectations	
SS		
MS		
3,551	heightened interest in	
SS		
MS		
3,552	resonate with	
SS		
MS		

3,553	grind to a halt	
SS		
MS		
3,554	offer inducements	
SS		
MS		
3,555	general awareness	
SS		
MS		
3,556	in a bid to	
SS		
MS		
3,557	patrons of	
SS		
MS		
3,558	repeated allegations	
SS		
MS		

3,559	claim to be	
SS		
MS		
3,560	a force for good	
SS		
MS		
3,561	struggling towards	
SS		
MS		
3,562	link hands with	
SS		
MS		
3,563	arrogate to	
SS		
MS		
3,564	unbelievable distress	
SS		
MS		

3,565	limited in duration	
SS		
MS		
3,566	beguiling questions	
SS		
MS		
3,567	set in motion	
SS		
MS		
3,568	in a holding pattern	
SS		
MS		
3,569	growing sense of dread	
SS		
MS		
3,570	just awful	
SS		
MS		

About the Author

Everett Ofori holds an MBA from Heriot-Watt University (Scotland, UK) and a Master of Science, Finance, from the College for Financial Planning, Colorado, USA. He teaches Public Speaking, Management, Marketing, and English for Specific Purposes (Business Writing, Medical Writing, Meeting Facilitation, etc.). Everett has helped hundreds of high school and university students around the world to improve their writing and grades. He has also worked extensively with business executives (including those at the C-level).

Everett has worked with clients/students from the following organizations and more:

• Accenture	• Actelion
• Asahi Kasei Medical	• Asahi Soft Drink Research, Moriya
• Astellas	• Barclays
• Becton Dickinson	• Chugai/Roche Pharmaceuticals
• Disney	• ExxonMobil
• Fujitsu	• Goldman Sachs
• Gyao (Yahoo Japan)	• Hitachi Design
• IIJ (Internet Initiative Japan)	• Johnson & Johnson (Janssen)
• L'Oreal	• McKinsey Japan
• Mitsubishi (Shoji)	• Moody's
• National Institute of Land and Infrastructure Management, Tsukuba, Japan (NILIM)	• Orix
• PriceWaterhouseCoopers (PWC)	• Recruit
• Sekizenkai Nursing School, Shimosoga, Kanagawa	• Sumisho
• Summit Agro International	• Sumitomo
• Suntory	• Tokyo International Business College, Asakusabashi, Tokyo
• W. L. Gore	• Yokohama Child Welfare College (Hoiku Fukushi), Higashi-Totsuka, Kanagawa

www.ingramcontent.com/pod-product-compliance
Lightning Source LLC
Chambersburg PA
CBHW080020110526
44587CB00021BA/3416